Understanding Accounts

F. A. J. Couldery, FCA, FCIS, FHKSA

The Chartered Institute of Bankers

The Chartered Institute of Bankers
Emmanuel House
4–9 Burgate Lane
Canterbury
Kent
CT1 2XJ
United Kingdom

ISBN 0-85297-483-3

Designed by Geoff Green
Printed in Great Britain

Contents

Acknowledgments

I am grateful to The Chartered Institute of Bankers for permission to reproduce in Chapter 13 questions originally set in their examinations in accountancy at the lower level. They have been slightly modified to show them in modern format, but the answers are mine alone.

F. A. J. C.

1 The balance sheet

Balance sheets are probably one of the world's most widely known yet least understood documents. Ask anyone if they have heard of a balance sheet and the answer must be 'Yes'. Ask anyone other than an accountant (or, one hopes, a banker) to describe it, and one might as well seek guidance on black holes in space. Possibly people are better informed on the latter, because they are interesting and get talked about on television. When did you last see a balance sheet on television?

So what is a balance sheet? Is it really the document which tells one everything about the finances of a business? Does it reveal its business secrets? Is it the most important piece of paper related to a business? Does it show whether the business is going to succeed or fail? To all of these questions one can answer both 'Yes' and 'No'.

In its simplest form, a balance sheet is merely a list of all the good and bad things about a business. The 'goodies' are the things which have value – they are called the assets. The 'baddies' are the liabilities – the amounts owing to other people. Hopefully, the 'goodies' outnumber the 'baddies' and the excess is the capital or wealth of the proprietor. The principle is the same whether the proprietor is a single person (the sole trader), two or more people jointly owning the business (a partnership), or a company which has been created by some legal process and is really an artificial person. The last named is artificial in the sense that such a company has not (as a judge once put it) 'a body to be kicked or a soul to be saved' but is real enough in the eyes of the law in that it can own property and sue and be sued in the law courts.

Years ago, most balance sheets had two sides – one for the 'goodies' and one for the 'baddies'. The fashion today is to show balance sheets in vertical form, which is the format you will see in this book. In some cases the column is so long it has to be broken and spread over two pages, but it is still to be regarded as a vertical presentation and not a two-sided presentation. But remember that fashions change and that although UK companies currently favour vertical balance sheets and profit and loss accounts, you may well see US and French companies presenting the information in two-sided format.

Balance sheets are like snapshots of the business at a particular time – theoretically at one minute to midnight on the date shown. The date is important, for a balance sheet without a date would be like a railway timetable without dates – interesting as an academic exercise but quite useless for any practical purpose. Because of the difficulties often encountered in settling the figures in a balance sheet (e.g. valuation of the stock, liabilities to creditors, liability for taxation) it will usually be some days, weeks or even months after the balance sheet date that the balance sheet can be published – particularly if, as is the case with many private and all public companies, it also has to pass the scrutiny of the auditors who will examine the detail and report as to whether they find it 'true and fair'.

Balance sheet as at (date)

Fixed assets		X
Current assets	X	
Current liabilities	X	
Net current assets		X
Total assets less current liabilities		X
Deferred liabilities		X
Total assets less all liabilities		X
Representing:		
Capital		X

Figure 1. A balance sheet in outline

It will be seen that assets ('the goodies') come in two types – fixed assets and current assets. Fixed assets are not necessarily fixed in any geographical location: rather they should be thought of as being fixed in the balance sheet. Fixed assets are the assets which the company expects to retain long-term for the purpose of earning the profits. Thus they will include not only the freehold premises wherein the business activity is carried on, the plant and machinery used to manufacture goods and the office furniture and equipment, but also the motor vehicles used to transport both the goods and the salesmen (as well as the directors!). Current assets are defined as 'cash and assets held for conversion into cash'. The stocks of goods for resale and the debtors (who owe the business money for the goods and services they have bought from the business on credit terms) are the most usual items found in current assets.

Liabilities are also categorised into two groups: the current liabilities and the long term or deferred liabilities. Current assets are those that fall due for payment within one year of the balance sheet date. Since the Companies Act 1985 companies have actually had to spell out this definition in their balance sheet as 'Creditors: amounts falling due within one year'. Most current liabilities will have to be paid in much less than one year if trouble is to be avoided – e.g. will the telephone still be working in three months' time if BT have not been paid by then? Trade creditors (hopefully still showing their terms of business on statements as 'Net cash 30 days') and accrued expenses (i.e. costs for gas, water, electricity etc. used but not yet invoiced by the supplier) are the usual components of current liabilities. Bankers will know that bank overdrafts will also be shown under this heading, thanks to trade custom and a helpful High Court judge who concurred that such are repayable on demand.

Long term or deferred liabilities arise when a liability is repayable only after a longer period than one year – e.g. Debentures repayable in 10 years. Often a bank will make a loan to a company which is payable by instalments (with interest) over a period of, say, 20 years. In such cases the instalment which is repayable within the next year following the balance sheet debt will appear under current liabilities whilst the balance of the loan will be shown under the deferred heading (actually spelt out as 'Creditors: amounts falling due after more than one year').

The final section of the balance sheet, being the excess of total assets over total liabilities, is the capital of the proprietor, be that person an individual, a partnership or a company.

The items in more detail

Fixed assets will be shown under headings appropriate to the business, so that freehold premises, leasehold premises, plant and machinery, motor vehicles, etc. will appear in sub-totals. The law requires that companies segregate their tangible assets from their intangible assets: thus the former will be the premises and machinery, whilst the latter might include items such as goodwill, trade marks, patent rights. Whether the fixed assets are tangible or intangible, the accountancy profession has agreed on one important feature they all have: they have a limited economic life, that is to say, there is a limited period of time in which they will be of value to the business. Thus the buildings will be demolished, the lease will run out, the plant will wear out, and the vehicles will fail their MoT inspections! There is only one exception to this golden rule and that lies in freehold land (but not the buildings thereon). The Accounting Standards Committee (an important rule-making body formed by the leading professional bodies) ruled in 1977 that this is the only fixed asset which will not need depreciating – assuming always that it is not some mine nearing exhaustion or a crumbling coastal cliff!

Depreciation is the loss in value which fixed assets suffer through time, wear and tear and other causes such as changing technology. In practical terms, machinery may be expected to have a useful working life of 10 years, though computers are usually obsolete in three or four years. The expected useful life is therefore the period over which the cost (less any residual or scrap value) will be charged as an expense to the profit and loss account. It is important to recognise that although the total cost of the fixed asset will usually be paid in one sum (save when it is bought on hire purchase or instalment terms), it is shown as a fixed asset on the balance sheet until, year by year, the erosion in that asset value is recognised and a part of the cost is taken as an expense of each following year, with a corresponding reduction in the value shown in the balance sheet.

There are many ways of calculating depreciation, the main ones being described in Chapter 5.

Inflation is a complication in accounting statements, because it has the effect of reducing the value of the unit of measurement (the £) over time: thus £1,000 in 1990 has a different real value to £1,000 in 1995, but if the business spent such a sum in each year on machinery, it will report in its balance sheet 'Machinery at cost £2,000'. The accountancy profession has spent a great deal of energy trying to find a practical solution to this problem and more than one new set of accounting proposals have been hatched over the last 30 years: none have found much favour in practice – mainly because of the extra work they would involve and the limited understanding the public would have of them – and the only generally accepted outcome has been the realisation that if fixed assets are to be held long-term (e.g. freehold property or investments in company shares) they should be periodically revalued and the up-to-date figure taken into the balance sheet. An important point to remember here is that any surpluses so arising cannot be regarded as profits and company law forbids taking them to the profit and loss account: instead they must be recognised as 'unrealised gains' and taken to a separate account of the shareholders called 'Revaluation reserve', this title constituting a form of warning that subsequent revaluations may be in the opposite direction!

Current assets have to be valued afresh each year. The largest item is often stock, and the rule here is that one normally values at cost, because although it may be sold tomorrow at a profit it is always wrong in accountancy law to anticipate a profit: one values at cost and carries it forward on the basis that it is an expense incurred which is not yet matched to any corresponding revenue. It is possible, however, that the value of the stock has been reduced by factors such as obsolescence, deterioration, errors in production or just plain fashion. The rules here change, and whilst one never takes a future profit into account one does take a prospective loss into account (hence the accountant always being regarded as the born pessimist). If the expected sale price, net of selling expenses, is less than the original cost, one takes that former figure as the current value. This is known as the 'net realisable value'.

A similar principle applies with the valuation of debtors. One takes the invoiced selling price to the customer as the value of the debt, because although it will contain the profit on sale this is a realised profit and the invoice price can be the subject of a claim in the courts. However, if the debtor is insolvent or for any other reason is considered unlikely to pay the full debt, a provision for the bad or doubtful debt is made and the value shown in the balance sheet reduced accordingly. The accountant's pessimism pervades all accounting statements, so that he will always try to give early warning of bad news, even if at a later date he finds he can publish some better news.

Liabilities are shown at their full value, whether they are due for payment within one year or at a later date. It has been suggested that a debt not due for payment for some years should be shown at a discounted amount (because one could invest a lesser sum now which would, with interest, grow to make such sum in the future) but such discounting is rarely undertaken. Inflation would also imply that the size of a liability would effectively shrink over time, but again this is ignored.

Sometimes a business may have the possibility of a liability, rather than the certainty of one. An example would be where it had guaranteed the liability of another person, perhaps on a bank overdraft. A liability would only arise if and when that other person defaulted on his obligations. This is known as a 'contingent liability'. Contingent liabilities are not shown within a balance sheet but, if they could be material, they would be shown in a note attached to the balance sheet.

Capital

The capital in a business is shown in different forms, depending on the legal entity of that business.

The capital of a sole trader will be shown in one sum on the proprietor's capital account in the balance sheet. This figure will seldom remain constant, for it will increase in each accounting period by the net profit and also by any further funds brought into the business, and it will decrease by any net loss sustained and also by amounts withdrawn from the business (e.g. for living expenses):

the last mentioned are referred to as the proprietor's drawings and are always deducted from his capital account and *never* included as wages in the profit and loss account, even though the proprietor will often refer to such sums as his wages.

In a partnership, the only difference in the balance sheet is that each partner will have his own balance sheet entry or entries, showing his funds in the business. This may be simply an individual capital account, maintained on the same principles as that of the sole trader. Often, however, it is agreed that each partner shall maintain a fixed amount of capital (e.g. £10,000) and the excess or deficit is dealt with on a separate current account for each partner. In such cases the capital account will be left untouched each year and the current account will have the share of net profit for the partner added to it and his drawings deducted from it. The balance sheet will therefore show both a capital and a current account for each partner.

In the case of a company, the law requires that the share capital should be shown separately at all times. This is not necessarily the original sum subscribed when the company was formed as many companies will increase their share capital over the years, sometimes by selling more shares to their members (a 'rights issue') and sometimes by giving their members a free or 'bonus issue'. The latter is more correctly described as a 'capitalisation issue' as all it is doing is capitalising existing profits by transferring them from profit and loss account (whence they could be distributed as dividends) to share capital account (whence they could not). The profits not distributed as dividend are usually accumulated on profit and loss account (where they may be referred to as 'Retained profits') or they may be transferred to one or more so-called 'reserves' which are sometimes earmarked for particular purposes (e.g. dividend equalisation account, reserve for plant replacement). Such categorisation of reserves is now generally discouraged, but company law often requires the creation of a particular reserve and gives it a special function: the revaluation reserve mentioned above is one example, another is the share premium account which must be created when a company sells shares above their nominal value. By whatever names reserves may be known, it is the total of the share capital and all reserves which constitutes the full capital of

John Brown, grocer
Balance Sheet – 31 December 19..

	£	£
Fixed assets		
Leasehold premises at cost	20,000	
Less depreciation	8,250	11,750
Shop equipment and fittings at cost	11,500	
Less depreciation	8,360	3,140
		14,890
Current assets		
Stock	4,300	
Debtors and prepaid expenses	4,880	
Cash at bank and in hand	2,160	
	11,340	
Current liabilities		
Trade creditors	3,635	
Accrued expenses	1,620	
Bank overdraft	750	
	6,005	
Net Current Assets		5,335
Net assets		20,225
Capital account		
Balance brought forward	21,786	
Add Net profit for the year	22,548	
	44,334	
Less Drawings during year	24,109	20,225

Figure 2. A balance sheet of a sole trader

Addit & Checkit, accountants
Balance Sheet – 31 March 199..

	£	£
Fixed assets		
Motor cars at cost	35,700	
Less depreciation	8,650	27,050
Office equipment at cost	15,800	
Less depreciation	6,830	8,970
		36,020
Current assets		
Work in progress	13,650	
Debtors	9,520	
Cash	125	
	23,295	
Current liabilities		
Creditors	1,382	
Accrued expenses	830	
Bank overdraft	14,864	
	17,076	
Net current assets		6,219
Net assets		42,239
Capital accounts		
Addit	15,000	
Checkit	12,000	27,000
Current accounts		
Addit	12,473	
Checkit	2,766	15,239
		42,239

Figure 3. A balance sheet of a partnership

Big Town Trading Co Ltd
Balance Sheet – 30 June 19..

	£	£
Fixed assets		
Tangible fixed assets	264,700	
Investments	9,692	274,392
Current assets		
Stocks	175,900	
Debtors	85,793	
Cash	3,781	
	265,474	
Creditors: amounts falling due within one year		
Creditors	164,805	
Corporation tax	74,640	
Bank overdraft	27,894	
	267,339	
Net Current Liabilities		(1,865)
Total assets less current liabilities		272,527
Creditors: amounts falling due after more than one year		
9% Debentures 2010		100,000
Net assets		172,527
Capital and reserves		
Called up share capital	50,000	
Revaluation reserve	27,800	
General reserve	50,000	
Retained profits	44,727	172,527

Figure 4. A balance sheet of a company

the company and it is important to remember that creditors always have priority over shareholders in a winding up, and no shareholder is entitled to anything on such an occasion until and unless all creditors have been paid in full: only at that stage does one have to go into the finer detail and consider whether one group of shareholders may have a prior claim over another group, e.g. if there are both preference and ordinary shares in issue.

Illustrations of a simple balance sheet of a sole trader, a partnership and a limited company are shown in Figures 2, 3 and 4 respectively. The latter uses the jargon and format laid down in the Companies Act 1985, albeit in a simplified style.

Note that whilst it is customary to show most of the detail within the balance sheet of a sole trader or a partnership (as with the figures of cost and depreciation of fixed assets), in the case of companies there is now so much detail which company law requires to be shown that the fashion has developed of showing only the main figures on the face of the balance sheet with all the detail in the pages of notes which follow that document. Thus the manner in which the figure for tangible fixed assets is derived will be explained in great detail, showing not only the classes of assets but which have been subject to revaluation and how much depreciation has been provided thereon. The changes in these figures between one year and another also have to be provided.

Finally, a mark earning point for examinations. Balance sheets show a 'snapshot' view of a business at a particular date. It is vital to state that date, for without it the document is as useless as a bus timetable without dates. Many candidates lose a mark or two by forgetting to put the date on their balance sheet, and that is often the difference between a pass and a fail in an examination.

2 The profit and loss account

If one merely wishes to determine the amount of profit or loss made by a business in a given period, it can be done by the use of balance sheets alone. Taking the case of John Brown, grocer, as an example (Figure 2, Chapter 1) we might determine that at 31 December 19.1, his net assets had risen from £20,225 the previous year to £24,750 – an increase of £4,525. We must now ask what capital he has added to the business or withdrawn from it during the year. If he has added nothing but withdrawn £25,000 for personal use, then the net profit must have been £4,525 plus £25,000, a total of £29,525.

Sometimes, as where adequate records have not been kept, this method of determining the profit of the year is the only one available, and Inspectors of Taxes frequently use it! However, much greater information is desirable and with proper records of transactions this is shown as a profit and loss account (Figure 5).

In the above case, had the business been that of a sole trader the net profit of £102,191 would have been carried to the capital account, thereby increasing it, though drawings would then decrease the balance on that account. As this is a partnership, however, the profit earned by the firm must be split between the partners and this is shown as a 65/35 split. Partnership law states that the partners may share profits in any way they choose, and only in the absence of any previous agreement will the law impose an equal division between the partners (on the basis that such an apportionment would seem less unfair than any other method). In practice, the ways in which partners share profits can be extremely complicated, involving giving the partners interest on their capital accounts, charging it on their drawings, giving them individual

Addit & Checkit, accountants
Profit and loss account
Year ended 31 March 19..

	£	£
Fees receivable		235,918
Less expenses:		
Staff salaries	95,729	
Rent and rates	12,609	
Lighting and heating	3,711	
Professional subscriptions	2,058	
Bank charges	2,715	
Travelling expenses	7,276	
General expenses	3,713	
Depreciation, motor cars	3,740	
Depreciation, office equipment	2,176	133,727
Net profit for the year		102,191
Net profit divided:		
Addit – 65%	66,424	
Checkit – 35%	35,767	102,191

Figure 5. A profit and loss account of a partnership

salary amounts and only then going on to a fractional or percentage basis of dividing what is left. Many of these complications arise from the fact that in the professions it is now possible to have literally hundreds of partners sharing a common fund of profit, but happily one may still find others who are content to divide the profit equally.

In the case of companies, company law has decreed the format of the profit and loss account as well as that of the balance sheet, and an illustration of this is given in Figure 6.

As was the case with the company balance sheet, company

Big Town Trading Co Ltd
Profit and Loss Account
Year ended 30 June 19..

Turnover		1,289,962
Less Cost of sales		941,653
Gross profit		348,309
Less Distribution costs	42,907	
Administrative expenses	218,600	261,507
Net profit before taxation		86,802
Taxation:		
Corporation tax at 21%		15,360
Net profit after taxation		71,442
Dividends:		
Interim – paid	20,000	
Final – proposed	30,000	50,000
Retained profits for the year		21,442
Retained profits brought forward		23,285
Retained profits carried forward		44,727

Figure 6. A profit and loss account of a company

profit and loss accounts are now little more than summary statements, with none of the detail we get in the profit and loss account of a sole trader or partnership. One reason for this is that company accounts have to be filed each year with the Registrar of Companies, from whom anyone may obtain copies on payment of a small fee. (Small companies are allowed to file the barest figures only, using the balance sheet without any profit and loss account.) In all cases, much detail is given in the form of notes.

Turnover does have a statutory definition – briefly, it means total sales for the period – but most of the other jargon used is open to individual interpretation by companies. Thus 'Cost of sales' is assumed by most people to mean simply the cost of goods sold, i.e. purchases for the year adjusted by opening and closing stocks. However, although small companies invariably adopt that meaning we find that in the accounts of supermarkets such expression can also include the cost of staff, premises and all related expenses at the branches. Similarly, 'Distribution costs' and 'Administrative expenses' can be compressed or stretched as desired. In total, however, all the operating expenses of the company (including depreciation) have to be fitted into one of those three headings.

The law has required certain items, including directors' remuneration, loan interest and depreciation, to be disclosed, and again such disclosure in found in the notes rather than on the face of the profit and loss account.

Company directors often talk about 'ploughing back profits', perhaps giving the uninitiated an image of them rising at an early hour, harnessing the horses and going out into the fields to do hard manual labour under the heat of the sun. Nothing could be further from the truth! The retained profits shown at the foot of the profit and loss account are simply those profits not being taken by the Inland Revenue as tax or the shareholders as dividend. They are 'ploughed back' by doing nothing more with them!

Retained profits form part of the reserves of the company, which were mentioned in the last chapter. People often think of a company's reserves as being chests full of money stashed away in a bank vault to provide salvation when disaster strikes. Reserves could conceivably (if improbably) take such a form, but will usually be represented by more assets, be they tangible or intangible, fixed or current. Reserves form part of the long-term shareholders' funds in the business: they can be very beneficial to a company – from what other source could one obtain long-term capital without having to pay interest charges?

Dates again are important. A profit and loss account is usually for a period of one year, which must be specified. Sometimes a bank will seek a profit and loss account for a shorter period, e.g. three months or a half-year, from a sole trader or a partnership. Such a request always indicates a worried banker – worried that the business may not last out the full year!

3 Fundamental accounting concepts

The somewhat formidable title to this chapter is how the accountancy profession refers to its basic 'rules of the game'.

Accountancy, as the reader will discover, is far more than merely adding a few figures together and putting them in the right place. Academics like to argue about whether accountancy is an art or a science: most accountants, if they could understand what distinction the academic was trying to make, would no doubt end up believing that it must be a bit of both! Even when all the detailed transactions of a business have been faithfully recorded, day by day, they must then be summarised under appropriate headings and there is still much skill and judgment needed in drawing conclusions as to the overall effect of a year's operations on a business. Although there is a broad area of general agreement among accountants, it is not much of an exaggeration to say that, particularly in the case of a company which was 'just keeping its head above water', one accountant would produce accounts showing a net profit whilst another accountant would produce accounts for the same period showing a net loss.

There are bound to be matters over which individual views must differ, e.g. the value of unsold stock, the likelihood of some debts proving to be irrecoverable, the amount which should be set aside for warranty claims on products sold.

However, it is an established rule within the accountancy profession (SSAP 2) which has now been taken into the Companies Act 1985 that four rules must be observed in all published accounts *unless it is otherwise expressly stated*. These four are described as being fundamental accounting concepts and are the concepts of going concern, accruals, consistency and prudence.

Going concern concept

This assumes that the business will be continuing its activities for the foreseeable future on a similar scale. There are many factors which cause an enterprise to close, the two most frequent being lack of money and lack of management, though others as diverse as road diversions, changes in law, opening of competing businesses and changes in fashion can have the same effect.

If by reason of trading losses being sustained, for example, a business has lost so much money that it is going to be difficult to carry on its trade, it may mean that normal trading must cease. In this event, stock may have to be disposed of in the trade or at greatly reduced prices, possibly below cost. Similarly, fixed assets having a special purpose (e.g. computer controlled milling machines) may no longer have a useful function and may be worth only scrap value. Finally, when any business closes there is the burden of redundancy payments to staff.

In the case of a small business, the death of the prime mover (who is usually the owner, but may be a manager) may well entail the death of the business, since there will be difficulties in finding an immediate successor. Thus an accountant in practice may employ accounting and secretarial staff, but the business cannot continue without a qualified professional man at the top. Similar situations arise in most professions, from actuaries to veterinary surgeons. For these reasons, a small business must always be more vulnerable than a large one.

Unless otherwise stated, therefore, one may assume that those who have drawn up the accounts have consciously thought about whether there may be any obstacles to the continuation of the business and have concluded that there are not. The values attaching to assets and liabilities in the balance sheet are sometimes said to reflect the 'going concern' value, as distinct from the 'gone concern' one meets in bankruptcy, where asset values plunge and liabilities seem to multiply.

Recent Auditing Standards published by the profession require an auditor to consider in depth (and record his reasoning) whether the business will be able to continue as a going concern for a minimum of 12 months after the date of his audit report. Since the continued support of a banker is often vital to achieve such a view, the auditor is expressly invited to have a tripartite meeting with his client and the banker if there is doubt on the point.

Accruals concept

There are very few businesses where all trading is conducted for cash. Most High Street shops insist on cash (or plastic cards, the modern form of cash) and do not give credit to customers, but they seldom have to pay for their purchases instantly on receipt, nor do they pay their expenses daily: such services as gas, electricity and telephone (to name but three) are all on the usual quarterly accounts, and even their staff do not get paid more often than once a week or month.

If one attempted to measure profit or loss merely by looking at the cash transactions, one would never see a true picture, for one would not bring into the reckoning any expenses which had not yet been paid for, and one might well include cash payments for benefits which had all been received in the previous accounting period.

What is vital to any accurate assessment of profit or loss for an accounting period is the matching of total costs incurred on the one hand with total revenue obtained on the other hand. Whether some of the costs have not yet been reflected by cash passing is largely irrelevant: no employee would consider he had wasted the first 29 days in a month simply because he did not receive his month's salary until the 30th day.

It is often convenient, from a book-keeping point of view, to start with the total figure of payments for a period, but one must bring into account, or 'accrue', payments which have not yet been made but relate to the period under review. Thus one brings in creditors for purchases, accrued liabilities for gas, electricity, telephone charges and (one hopes) accountancy fees. Similarly, one brings in debtors for sales made and services rendered.

It is also important to remember that one sometimes has to pay in advance for some items, e.g. insurance and business rates. In such cases, one needs to carry forward a part of the payment (usually on a time basis) so that part of the cost is shown in the next period's accounts, which is the period in which the rest of the benefit will be received.

In a very few instances, a summary of the cash transactions of an organisation may suffice: clubs may sometimes present a 'receipts and payments' account and in such cases there may be no outstanding debtors or creditors to accrue. In all major cases, however, it is essential to appreciate that one is bringing into account (by accruing that which is not yet paid or received) the full costs incurred and the total benefits obtained by an enterprise in its accounting period.

Consistency concept

An old saying in accountancy runs 'It is better to be consistent than precise'. In practice, one tries to be both, but one has to admit that consistency is even more vital than precision. For example, if one were consistently to count '1-2-4-5-8-9-10' one would be able to establish whether (for example) sales had been greater this year than last, and whether stock had increased. However, if one sometimes counted '1-2-8-9-5-4-10' it would be futile to attempt to arrive at any conclusions.

Unless one is consistent, not merely in one's actual counting, but also in the way one proceeds to value assets and liabilities, one is on dangerous ground in attempting to draw any conclusions or comparisons at all. Thus, valuing the stock at cost price one year and at selling price the next year would be a certain recipe for false accounts.

Sometimes one has a situation in which changed circumstances (or perhaps just technical enlightenment) make it desirable to vary one's approach to an accounting problem. A change in the way of arriving at a stock valuation, or an alteration to one's approach to depreciation, may be the result. The consistency concept does not prevent one making a change. What it does do is to make it necessary to draw attention to the changed approach and to calculate and show the effect of making such a change. In other words, one sees in the accounts a plainly marked item showing the impact of the alteration, which is usually described as a change of accounting policy. Without such an item on the face of the accounts, one is entitled to assume that no such changes have taken place and that comparisons with earlier periods are valid.

Prudence concept

It is sometimes suggested that accountants are the world's worst pessimists. Say 'Good morning' to an accountant – so the legend runs – and he will probably answer 'Yes it is, but I think we'll have some rain later'.

The one word 'prudence' is a convenient way to sum up the cautious way in which an accountant approaches his task of declaring a profit or a loss. It is, at root, a basic rule that requires him to bring into account a possible loss, but to leave out of account a possible profit until it has been made.

If prudence means that he has to be a pessimist (and it probably does mean just that), it is certainly not a fault for which the accountant need apologise. The business world is seemingly full of bright young whiz kids who do not hesitate to assure everyone that they will change the world, at latest by 4 o'clock tomorrow afternoon. The accountant, by comparison, may clomp about in his lead boots, but if it keeps his feet on the ground and stops him joining those who have their head in the clouds it is not necessarily a bad thing. One does not have to apologise if a profit which has been shown at £3,000 turns out to be one of £4,000. But if one has forecast a material profit when the actual events deliver a nasty loss, something more than apologies are sometimes needed, for someone somewhere has to suffer that loss.

Accountants often complain that they need the astrologer's crystal ball to foretell the future, but such useful accessories are not often available from office furnishers. Erring on the side of caution must be the rule in cases of doubt: prudence is not merely desirable – it is little short of vital in the field of accounting.

Financial reporting standards

There is a stream of fresh thought continuously pouring from one committee or another on what is proper, necessary or desirable to be shown in accounting statements. At the time of writing, the latest series of rules for the accountancy profession is entitled 'Financial Reporting Standards'. These are adding to, modifying and sometimes contradicting the earlier series of "'Statements of Standard Accounting Practice'. Other bodies also try to get in on the act, the latest being the Charity Commission who now insist that even if a charity is a registered company it should publish a financial statement known as a 'Statement of Financial Activities' which has little in common with a profit and loss account (or an income and expenditure account, as non-profit-making bodies normally call them). As a result of all this activity it will be realised that fashion applies to many things in addition to ladies' clothing! Supplementary schedules to the main accounting statements seem to be the order of the day, ranging from a summary cash flow statement to an analysis of the directors' remuneration, from a summary of recognised but unrealised gains to a list of transactions undertaken by a company with related parties (as defined).

Only the professional accountant must try to keep abreast of these changing conventions, but the basic rules affecting balance sheets and profit and loss accounts do not vary. One of the early decisions of the profession (1971) was that figures alone are not enough and explanations as to how the figures have been constructed are required. This was SSAP 2, which required the disclosure of accounting policies.

Accounting policies

Compliance with the four fundamental accounting policies described above is a start to the rigid framework within which company accounts are now constructed, but by themselves alone are not sufficient to explain the figures. Within each company, the directors (in theory, but in practice the chief accountant) will decide how detailed matters on the accounts proceed. For example, how should depreciation be calculated? (There are many different ways, as Chapter 5 will show.) How should the profits on long-term contracts be apportioned to different accounting periods? What should be done with the profits and losses arising from fluctuating exchange rates on overseas business? Is it desirable or necessary to provide for future taxation, and if so on what basis? When should the company write off its expenditure on research and development? These are but a sample of the problems to which each company may have to find a solution, and whilst there are many guidelines established, there are no rigid rules applicable to all cases.

The decisions made within each company are known as its accounting policies. Most importantly, they are not merely made but published each year with the annual accounts. Thus, before making comparisons between two apparently similar companies, you need to read the page of accounting policies of each. Clearly if one company is adopting a heavier charge for depreciation (e.g. writing off machinery over five years, whilst the other is writing off over 10 years), that company will be reducing its profits more in the short-term, though the benefit may show in year six, when the machinery is fully written off but is still in use.

The requirement in SSAP 2 is that accounting policies must be disclosed for those matters 'which are judged material or critical in determining profit or loss for the year and in stating the financial position'.

The moral is simple. In studying annual accounts, read the words before the figures.

True and fair view

Before the Companies Act 1948 (a forerunner of the 1985 Act) came into force, the legal requirement was that a company's balance sheet should show a 'true and correct' view. A subtle but far-reaching change introduced by the 1948 Act was that the words became 'true and fair'.

At first sight this seems to be playing with words – an exercise in semantics, as the Americans are fond of saying. In practice, it has brought about a much more honest and well-considered presentation of facts.

Directors and auditors alike could previously shelter behind the 'true and correct' label on the grounds that the figures were shown as they appeared in the books and that the balance sheet was a summary of those books. Once the concept of fairness is introduced, however, one has to ask whether the picture so presented is a reasonable portrayal of the underlying facts. Is it fair to show fixed assets written down to £1 when the directors know that one property alone is worth £250,000? Is it fair to put a figure of £75,000 on an item of stock which has proved unsaleable?

A balance sheet may have many basic faults in its construction, which are the subject of comment elsewhere in this book, but although it can never be all things to all men (and one single document can seldom satisfy the different needs of the creditor, the banker and the tax inspector – to name but three people), the one feature which is now indisputable about balance sheets is that they must not be constructed in such a way as to mislead. Fair in detail and fair in overall impression is the overriding consideration, and when the auditor certifies that in his opinion the accounts show a true and fair view he knows that he cannot rely upon mere mathematical precision in stating that view.

Materiality

Although the world may have a picture of an accountant as being a person who is obsessed with fine detail, this is not a 'true and fair' view, for one basic principle is that he should not get immersed in detail to the detriment of the overall picture. As the accountant puts it, he does not bother with amounts unless they are 'material'. What is and what is not 'material' is a point on which many views are possible, but even if the borderline is not well defined, the principle is clear to see. Two examples may help.

In Figure 3, Chapter 1, suppose when the accountant went to check the £125 cash balance he found a note saying that one of the staff had borrowed £50. What should he do? If the cash left is only £75 it would seem wrong to overstate it as £125: should not debtors be increased by £50 and cash reduced by this amount? The amount is not large, but is it material? Probably today one would conclude that it was not, and the cash balance would be left showing as £125 if the loan was promptly repaid by the member of staff.

In the balance sheet of the company (Figure 4, Chapter 1), suppose that one of the debtors who owed £100 had actually paid the debt but that this receipt had not been recorded until the following day and the money had been left in a drawer overnight. Should some adjustment be made to debtors and cash figures? Strictly the answer should be yes, but in relation to the figures in the balance sheet the sum involved is not material and the entry could well be left until the following day.

Junior staff often get confused because some small items are considered important whilst others are not. Such matters as honesty and truth are important, and if the sums of £50 or £100 have been stolen then the facts must be reported. One cannot condone dishonesty on the grounds that it was only a small sum in relation to what was there! What the principle of materiality is about is whether it is necessary or desirable to go to a lot of work to show fine detail when the overall view is still the same. It always costs money to get detail, and one must keep a sense of proportion and realise that if, as often happens, the final accounts are published to the nearest £1,000 it is futile to spend time arguing about £100 on bad debt provisions.

The author is old enough now to tell a story against himself without feeling too embarrassed. As a newly qualified chartered accountant, I was working in the City of London as an audit manager for a firm of chartered accountants. The client was an international oil company, and on the second day of the audit I discovered an error of over £12,000 in the calculations of stock value. In haste, I left the client's premises to see the senior partner and report this major mistake. 'It's not material, lad' said the partner, 'go back and get on with the audit!' About to protest that £12,000 was a big sum, I remembered just in time that I had been told the previous day that, for the first time ever, the client's accounts were to be published that year to the nearest million pounds.

4 The distinction between capital and revenue

One fundamental distinction which is vital to any understanding of accounts is the difference between capital and revenue expenditure.

Capital expenditure is that which gives a long term benefit to the business. It frequently results in the acquisition of a tangible fixed asset, such as a building, a machine or a vehicle. The fixed asset will usually lose most if not all of its value over a period of years, as explained in Chapter 5, Depreciation. But it is also possible to incur capital expenditure which is not represented by an tangible asset, e.g. the acquisition of patent rights, or the purchase of goodwill.

Since capital expenditure, by definition, will give a lasting benefit to the business, it would be unreasonable to charge all the cost against the income of the year of acquisition. Although the full purchase price will usually have to be found in cash at one time, it is obvious that the cost should be spread over the period during which benefits will be obtained. This is the function of depreciation.

Capital expenditure is therefore normally carried to the balance sheet as a fixed asset, and unless we are buying freehold land (which is now regarded as the only asset capable of having ever-lasting value), we expect to see the balance sheet value decrease over the period of its useful life.

By contrast, revenue expenditure is that which buys instant but not long-lasting benefits. Such expenses as staff wages, lighting and heating costs, bank charges, accountancy fees, are all items which will constantly recur. The benefit from the expenditure is obtained in that particular week, month or (exceptionally) year in which the payment is made or the expense incurred. Revenue expenditure is therefore written off as an expense in the period to which it relates, and the only adjustment we have to make is the adjustment to carry forward unused benefits (e.g. prepaid insurance) or to bring in charges not yet invoiced (e.g. accrued telephone call charges): apart from such adjustments, all revenue expenditure will be charged to the profit and loss account of the year.

Deferred revenue expenditure

Exceptionally, one may encounter a hybrid form of expense, known as deferred revenue expenditure. A company may embark on an elaborate advertising campaign to promote some new product. It may reason that the benefits from this expense will not all be received in the immediate future, but may be spread over one or two years to come. Similarly, travel agencies are expected to have lavish full-colour brochures printed describing their package holidays. They might print enough to last for two years, keeping the price list on a separate insert which could be changed as often as necessary. In these and similar cases, it can be argued that some of the costs should be carried forward and set against the benefits which will be received in later periods. Any such carry-forward will obviously lighten the expenses to be set against this year's income (increasing this year's profit or diminishing this year's loss), with a corresponding increase in next year's expenses (when the remainder of the expense will normally be charged).

Although the logic of carrying forward such deferred revenue expenditure cannot be faulted, accountants invariably frown on such a process. Unlike capital expenditure on a vehicle or some machinery which will obviously have some value in the future, even if the fixed asset is not used in the business as originally planned, deferred revenue expenditure may well give no benefits at all to future periods. If we have misjudged the market and the new product is a flop, or if the travel agency has organised a package holiday to a place where no one wishes to go (or where the hotel has burnt down), the whole of the expenditure will be money ill-spent and we will find that we have carried forward in the balance sheet a fictitious asset.

Deferred revenue expenditure can be found in balance sheets, and expenditure on the development of new products in the aerospace and electronics industries are good examples, but the overall view is that a healthy business is expected, by and large, to take such expenses in its stride and write them off as expenses of the period in which they are incurred. Unless the expenditure is major (and developing a new aircraft is extremely expensive), carrying forward such items rather gives the impression that one is 'scraping the bottom of the barrel' to make a current year's results look better than they otherwise would do. Where major development expenditure is carried forward, an accounting standard (SSAP 13) applies which requires that only development expenditure (as distinct from research expenditure) is carried forward. It also makes the accountant apply several tests designed to minimise both the amount of such carry-forward and also the risks that the carry-forward is based on unreasonable optimism.

Receipts

Just as expenditure must be classified as capital or revenue, so it is necessary to distinguish between those receipts which relate to capital and those which are revenue by nature.

Capital receipts (sometimes confusingly referred to as 'capital income') are those which result from the disposal of a fixed asset (e.g. sale of a motor car) or from some other once-and-for-all item. In other words, they relate to matters that are not part of the normal trading activities of the business. Compensation for the compulsory purchase of part of one's land, or for the sale of technical knowledge ('know-how') are examples.

Capital receipts do not necessarily imply an automatic surplus or gain, for there is often an associated book value of a fixed asset to be adjusted as a result. If the compensation for compulsory purchase of one's land involved losing all one's land, the book value would have to be eliminated: only if the compensation exceeded the book value to be written off could one think in terms of a surplus. Where a partial disposal is involved, deciding by how much the book value should be adjusted can be a difficult problem, for it is not necessarily simply the amount of the compensation received.

A company can distribute any realised gain to its shareholders as dividends, regardless of whether the gain arose from an income receipt or a capital receipt. Although there have been several notable exceptions in recent years, few companies distribute gains arising from capital items, and such a gain is usually carried forward as a permanent addition to the capital of the business: if shareholders are to receive dividends, the source is invariably trading profits.

Revenue receipts (usually shortly known as income) are those which arise from the conduct of the business. They may range from the selling price of a bar of chocolate in a sweet shop, to a fee for services rendered by a professional person, to an admission fee received by a theatre. Such income is clearly in relation to goods or services currently being supplied, and should be recorded in the profit and loss account.

At first, the distinction between capital receipts and income appears precise and clear-cut. In practice there are so many ways in which money may become payable by one person to another that it is inevitable that we meet borderline cases. These often erupt as arguments with the Inland Revenue over the taxation of the gain, since capital gains are taxed under a different regime to revenue gains, and the taxpayer will obviously look at the alternative treatment and try to ensure the least painful one applies.

It is a safe rule in accountancy that if there is doubt over whether a receipt is capital or revenue, we treat it as a capital receipt and add it to reserves in the case of a company; but if one is in doubt about the nature of an expense, we write it off as an expense of the current period.

Above all, we try not to bury such items within other figures, unless the amount is not material. Full and precise information should always be given. If there is no short label to put on it, we give the details in a note referenced to the item. In today's fashion, the balance sheet and profit and loss account are easily fitted on a single page apiece, but the notes run for many pages.

5 Depreciation

If you ask a book-keeper 'What is depreciation?' you would probably be told 'It's the way the accountant writes off the cost of a fixed asset over its life'. Fixed assets, in common with us, usually end up being worn out. Machinery, motor vehicles, even buildings, all lose their value as time goes on and eventually have to be replaced. Sometimes there will be a scrap or residual value. If so, an estimate of this amount (if any) deducted from the original cost will give us the effective cost of the fixed asset. Over the estimated life of the asset, this is the amount which must be written off as a cost against income.

The accountant now has to use a more formal definition which he is given in SSAP 13. This is that 'Depreciation is the measure of the wearing out, consumption or other reduction in the useful economic life of a fixed asset whether arising from use, effluxion of time or obsolescence through technological or market changes'. Further, that 'The useful economic life of an asset is the period over which the present owner will derive economic benefits from its use'.

We therefore have one fact (the cost), two guesses (what residual value? what life?) and a problem – in what manner shall we write this effective cost off as an expense of each year?

There are several widely used methods of spreading this cost over the years and these are described below. To show the effect of each method, a graph indicates how an asset, which had cost £1,000, was estimated to have a residual value of £100 and an effective life of six years, would be dealt with. The mathematics of some of these methods is elementary, whilst in others it is quite complex. What is important to recognise is that there is a systematic approach to the problem: the same method is used for that asset (or groups of assets) each year. The method adopted and the percentage rates or other details are published in the annual accounts as part of the Accounting Policies adopted by that company.

Sometimes it is suggested that a simpler method would be to show the market value each year. This would cause its own problems, e.g. who will say what its market value is? Market value can also vary with fashion, and the advent of a new model of car could create a big fall one year in the market value of an older car. The accountant's view is that market value is irrelevant during the working life of a fixed asset. The asset has been acquired for a specific purpose and only in exceptional circumstances (e.g. a quadrupling of market value through some scarcity, concurrent with a readily available alternative within the business to achieve the same production) would market value make a company change its original plans. Depreciation is not an attempt to keep abreast of the market: it is the apportionment of the asset's effective cost in a fair manner. Market value is only relevant when the asset is acquired (cost) and when its life is ended (residual value). Depreciation is not a precise prediction, and although for the purpose of illustration the examples given below are worked to the nearest whole number, in practice rates will usually be rounded to the nearest 5% and although some accountants try to be precise in their calculations, abating annual depreciation amounts into monthly instalments for the years of acquisition and disposal, the usual practice is to charge a full year's depreciation in the year of acquisition and no depreciation in the year of disposal.

Since depreciation is seldom if ever going to result in a written down value which matches the residual value (if any) obtainable on the market, we always expect to have to make an adjustment when we dispose of the asset. The difference between the written down value in the books and the actual value received on disposal will be described as a profit or loss on disposal or scrapping.

The reducing balance method

This is a somewhat inept title, since all methods of depreciation involve a reducing balance. A more descriptive title would be 'Constant percentage applied to the reducing balance', for that is how we calculate it. We select a percentage rate which, when applied to the cost in the first year and to the written down value in subsequent years, will reduce the asset to the expected residual value at the end of its estimated life.

In Figure 7, a rate of 32% is appropriate to reduce the £1,000 cost to the £100 residual value at the end of six years.

It will be seen from the figures in the example that the depreciation charge is materially less in each successive year. The graph takes on the appearance of the flight path of an aircraft coming in to land – though if one is precise, it never does land, for the last £1 never gets written off and the asset cannot be given a nil value as is possible with other methods.

Several advantages are claimed for this method.

In the first place, it is invariably found that the older a machine is, the more it costs in repairs to keep it going. (If you doubt this, buy a motor car!) A diminishing depreciation charge coupled to an increasing repairs charge will therefore tend to give a more uniform annual cost of operating it, and this is considered realistic, since the value of the asset to the business each year is often the same, e.g. a seven-year-old bus earns just as much for the bus company as a one-year-old bus. (Some textbooks take this principle to the point of saying 'Charge revenue each year with a constant amount, and what is not spent on repairs is depreciation'. In practice, I still have to see this method used!

A second advantage is that the diminishing annual charge tends to reflect what is taking place with market values: it is often said that the greatest depreciation on a motor car takes place in the minute it takes to drive it out of the showroom, for thereafter it is a secondhand vehicle. However, remember that it is not a function of depreciation to mirror market value each year – all one is trying to do is to write off the effective cost of the asset to the business over its working life.

A third advantage for this method is that if we guess wrong on the expected life of the asset, it does not upset the calculations too badly. Whereas the straightline method (see Figure 9) would present us with problems if the asset survived for a seventh year, when using the reducing balance method it is simple to charge 32% of £100 and write the balance down to £68.

Cost		£1000
Year 1	32% x 1000	320
		680
Year 2	32% x 680	218
		462
Year 3	32% x 462	148
		314
Year 4	32% x 314	100
		214
Year 5	32% x 214	68
		146
Year 6	32% x 146	46
Residual Value		100

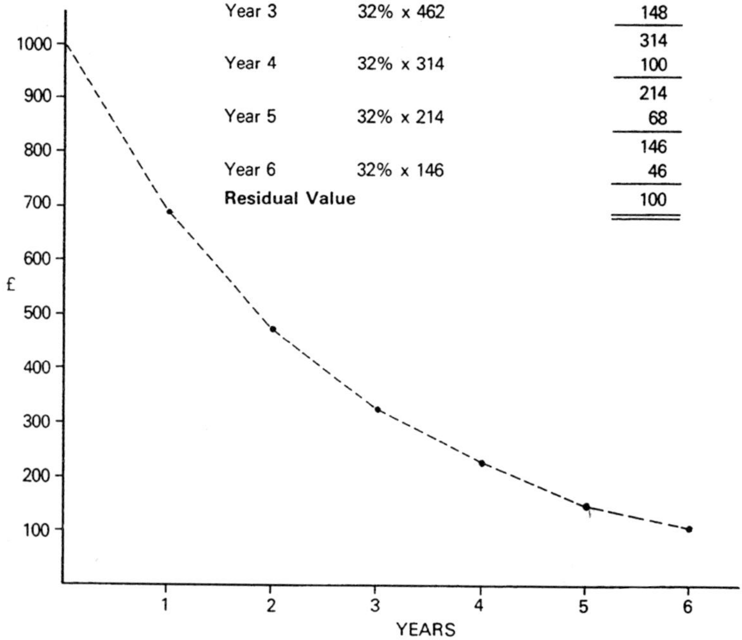

Figure 7. The reducing balance method

The sum-of-the-years method

As Figure 8 shows, this method gives a similar result to the reducing balance method, but the arithmetic is quite different.

The title suggests the technique. We estimate the effective life of the asset and if, as in this case, we decide it will be six years, we proceed to count 1 + 2 + 3 + 4 + 5 + 6 = 21. Using that total as the denominator, we reverse the numbering of the years and write off in Year 1 the fraction 6/21 of the effective cost, which in this case is (£1,000 – £100 =) £900.

Depreciation required in total is £1000 (cost) − £100 (residual value) = £900.

Cost		1000
Year 1	6/21 x 900	257
		743
Year 2	5/21 x 900	214
		529
Year 3	4/21 x 900	171
		358
Year 4	3/21 x 900	129
		229
Year 5	2/21 x 900	86
		143
Year 6	1/21 x 900	43
Residual Value		100
	21/21	

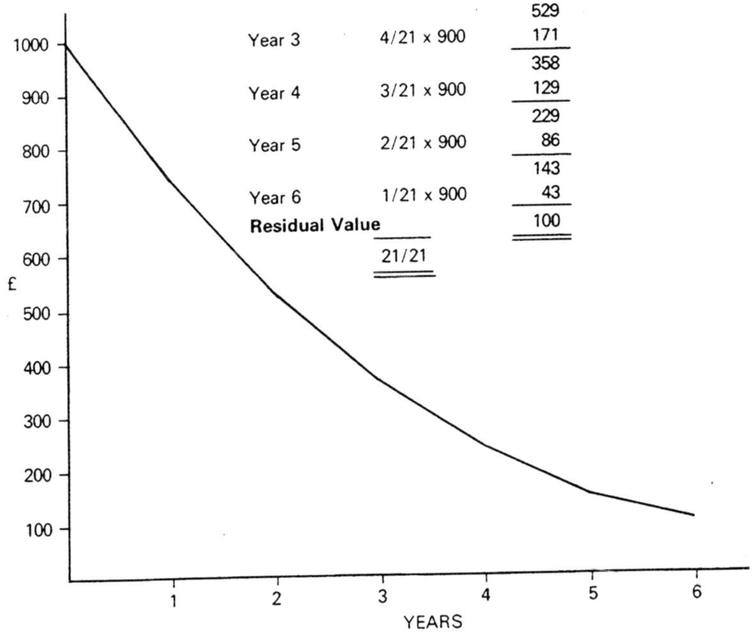

Figure 8. The sum-of-the-years method

The annual depreciation charge diminishes each successive year, giving the same advantages as are claimed for the reducing balance method.

The method has been widely used in the USA but only in recent years has it seen much use in the UK.

The straightline method

This is the method most widely used by large companies. It is

$$\textbf{Annual depreciation} = \frac{\text{Cost} - \text{Residual Value}}{\text{Effective Life}} = \frac{1000 - 100}{6} = 150$$

Cost	£1000
Year 1	150
	850
Year 2	150
	700
Year 3	150
	550
Year 4	150
	400
Year 5	150
	250
Year 6	150
Residual Value	100

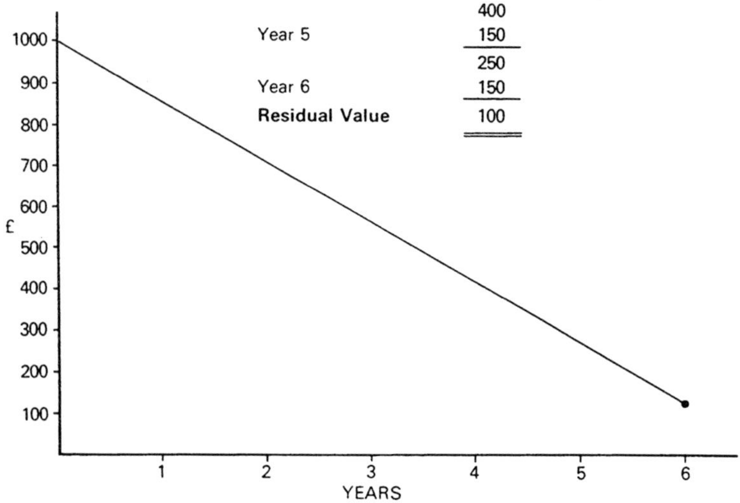

Figure 9. The straightline method

undoubtedly the simplest to use, which is probably the reason for its popularity.

We deduct from the cost of the asset its residual value (if any) and simply divide the balance by the effective life. We therefore get a constant annual charge for depreciation, and the shape of the graph obviously gives the method its name.

The straightline method is simple and easy to understand: having said that, it has no other claim to being scientific. Perfectionists argue at length that (as will be seen below) other methods take into account factors which should be incorporated in a depreciation system, but in the real world life must move on and simplicity is one of the greatest aids to progress. 'Keep it simple' is a cry made by many professionals, from engineers to tax inspectors!

The unit of depletion method

Sometimes the fixed asset to be depreciated is not an asset which has its life measured in units of time (e.g. a lease of property) but is in the nature of being a supply of a valuable commodity which may be used at fluctuating rates but is finite in quantity. Examples are quarries and oil wells, where the mineral supply may be abstracted at varying rates to suit the owner's needs. It may also be a machine whose effective life can be expressed in a number of running hours, and the example in Figure 10 shows such a case, where the machine's predicted life is 9,000 hours. In effect, we determine depreciation as being not a charge per year but as a charge per unit of output, the unit in this case being a machine hour.

Obviously the shape of the graph under this method can be anything from an 'L' to an inverted 'L'.

The advantage of this system is that the effective cost is clearly related to the benefits obtained by the business, and in cases where the unit of output is identifiable is it often the most appropriate method. It is widely used in cases of mineral extraction, including coal mines, and in the 19th century when many cemeteries were run as profit making public companies, it would also have been appropriate, though the name of the method may well have varied.

It might be thought suitable for other assets, e.g. could we use it for motor vehicles? If the vehicle is likely to achieve, say, 75,000 miles in its life, should we apportion 1/75,000th of the effective cost to each mile run? In such a case, we would merely look at the mileage reading to determine the amount of depreciation to charge in any year.

In practice this is seldom if ever done. Vehicles do not necessarily depreciate pro rata to the miles run. Time tends to be the dominant factor for depreciation with vehicles, though fashion, new models and even accident damage all contribute something. Low mileage second-hand cars do not fetch significantly more than those

Depreciation required in total (as before) £900

Estimated working life 9000 hours.

$$\text{Hourly rate} = \frac{£900}{9000} = £0.10$$

Cost		1000
Year 1	1000 hours at £0.10	100
		900
Year 2	1680 hours at £0.10	168
		732
Year 3	1260 hours at £0.10	126
		606
Year 4	2160 hours at £0.10	216
		390
Year 5	1480 hours at £0.10	148
		242
Year 6	1420 hours at £0.10	142
Residual Value		100
	9000	

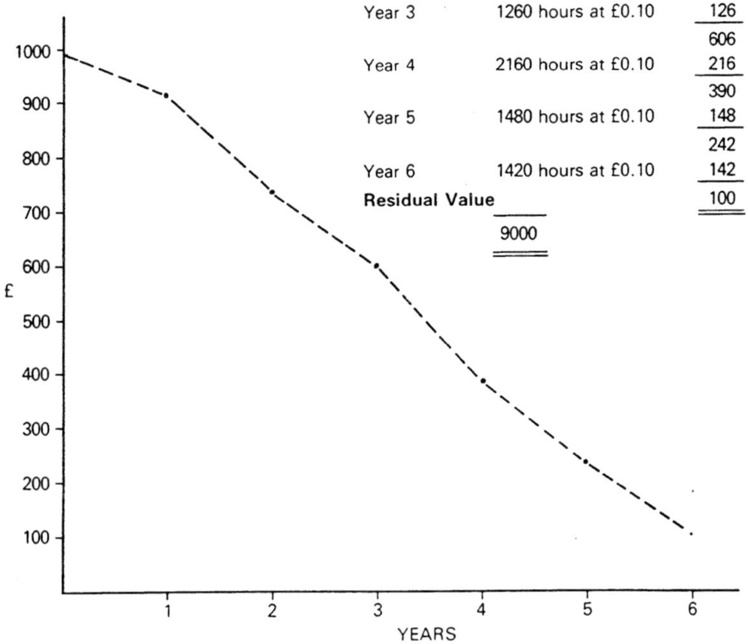

Figure 10. The unit of depletion method

whose mileage is greater, and the lack of availability of spare parts will often cause an old car to have little market value, irrespective of its condition or mileage run.

The revaluation method

Earlier in this chapter, I stressed that it is not the function of depreciation to try and match the book value with the market value

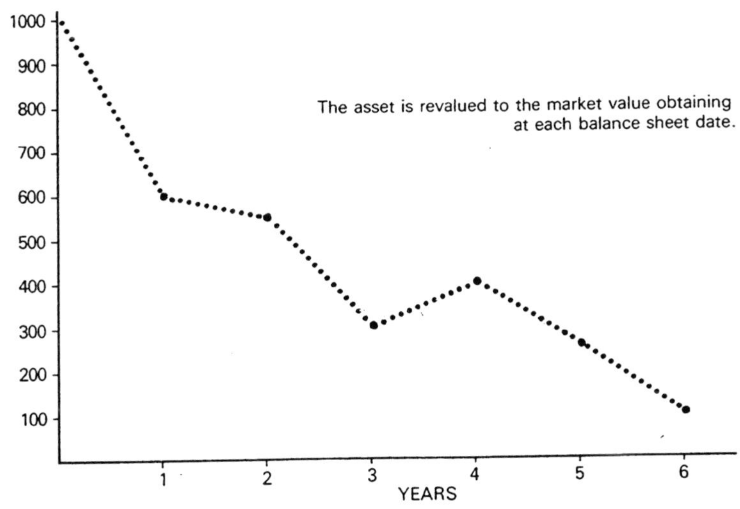

Figure 11. Revaluation

each year. I explained that this was not a suitable method for spreading the effective cost of an asset over its working life.

I now have to appear to contradict myself, for the method to be explained here does just that! It involves valuing the assets afresh each year and writing off any surplus amount standing on the books.

So what possible justification can there be for using such a method?

The answer is 'Simplicity'.

In many trades, from restaurants to engineering shops, there are numerous small items which are needed to run the business. The restaurants have glasses and cutlery, the engineering shops twist drills and hand tools. These all have one thing in common – these items get broken or taken! Whether the washing up machine is vicious on glasses or it is the customers who feel impelled to take a marked teaspoon home as a souvenir, the restaurant constantly keeps buying fresh supplies to ensure that there is a sufficient number of items available. And the same happens in the engineering works.

To try and record every breakage or loss would be an impossible task. As the items are not of great value, the simplest way is to add all new purchases to the book value of assets during the year, and, at the end of the year, count and value the survivors and write off as an expense any excess balance on the books.

Revaluation is not really a method but rather the simplest and cheapest solution to a difficult problem. It may result in showing appreciation (as in Year 4 in Figure 11): that is the price we pay for simplicity. But remember that it is only suitable for low value items. No bus company, buying double-decker buses at £65,000 apiece, would say 'Well, we started the year with 125 buses, but we've only got 122 at the balance sheet date'.

The annuity method

The annuity method introduces a concept known as 'opportunity cost' – a concept which would be better understood by most people if it were called 'the cost of lost opportunity'.

In effect, we say to the asset: 'You are a very expensive beast. Not only have you cost me £1,000, of which I shall only ever see £100 back, but in addition you have cost me the interest which I used to get whilst that £1,000 was invested in a savings account. Therefore, I am going to charge you that interest, and your depreciation will have to be increased to pay it'.

Before being able to calculate the depreciation, we must therefore know not only the cost, residual value and effective life of the asset, but also an appropriate interest rate to take into the calculations. In Figure 12, it has been taken as 20%, but in practice each company decides its own appropriate interest rate, which is usually referred to as its 'cost of capital'.

In the first year, we add to the cost an interest charge of 20% and deduct a constant amount (in this case £291). The net figure of depreciation resulting (£91) reduces the asset value to £909, and it is on this figure that interest is calculated the following year. Again the constant amount is written off. Because the interest figure must necessarily become smaller each year, though the constant amount

Cost			1000
Year 1	Interest at 20%	200 +	
	Constant amount	291 –	91
			909
Year 2	Interest at 20%	182 +	
	Constant amount	291 –	109
			800
Year 3	Interest at 20%	160 +	
	Constant amount	291 –	131
			669
Year 4	Interest at 20%	135 +	
	Constant amount	291 –	156
			513
Year 5	Interest at 20%	103 +	
	Constant amount	291 –	188
			325
Year 6	Interest at 20%	66 +	
	Constant amount	291 –	225
	Residual Value		100

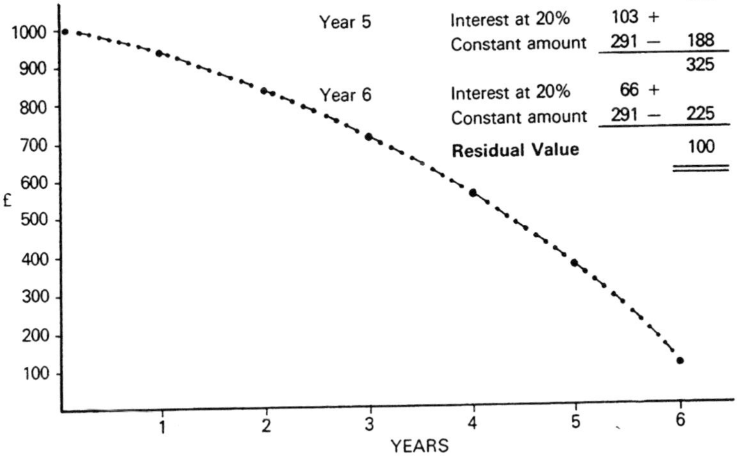

Figure 12. The annuity method

remains unchanged, the net figure of depreciation increases each year, giving the graph the distinctive shape shown – a stone thrown from the top of a tower.

In contrast to the other methods of depreciation, the mathematics of establishing this system can be complicated, for it will be realised that if we alter the constant 'minus' figure, we will automatically alter the interest 'plus' amount each year thereafter.

This method is considered appropriate for the depreciation of leases, and is in fact the method adopted by the Inland Revenue for computing the capital gains and losses on the disposal of wasting assets. To reduce the system to its simplest terms, the Finance Act 1965 (which introduced capital gains tax) contained a mathematical table showing the depreciation figures. In practice it is too complicated for most accountants to want to use, and the only real life application I have ever seen was by the Association of Certified Accountants in respect of its former premises in Bedford Square, London. (Unkind critics said their Council was merely showing off that they understood the system!)

The annuity method appeals to the academic accountant because, like the economist, he argues that interest foregone (the 'lost opportunity') is a real cost involved with fixed assets, even if one does not see it go out through the bank account. But accountants tend to be pragmatic animals and throughout the whole of accountancy we find a distinct dislike of bringing into account hypothetical costs, such as interest foregone. There have been whole generations of chartered accountants qualified who were no doubt delighted to find that economics was not a subject they had to study for their examinations!

Other aspects of depreciation

The foregoing methods by no means exhaust the ingenuity of accountants or mathematicians in devising ways of charging depreciation.

One further method involves a sinking fund, whereby one invests a constant sum each year outside the business: this sum builds up, with compound interest, to produce a sum sufficient to replace the asset. (At least that was the theory before inflation spoiled it!)

In another method, the business pays a constant annual premium on an endowment policy. In return, the insurance company promises to pay a predetermined sum at a fixed date in the future, which, so the theory goes, will be sufficient to pay for a replacement asset. (This method puts the uncertainty of interest rates onto the shoulders of the insurance company.)

Neither of these schemes finds many supporters. Most private companies do not have spare cash to invest outside the business for they are too busy trying to grow in size. The uncertainty introduced by inflation also detracts from any plan to 'save up' for replacement assets, and with the availability of several different methods for paying for the new asset when the time comes (including bank loans, hire purchase and finance leases), few small companies try to plan their finances years ahead.

A comparison of the methods already discussed in detail shows that although they all achieve their purpose over the life of the asset, there is an appreciable difference as to the impact on different years. Thus at the end of Year 3 the company using the reducing balance method would have charged £686 against its revenue for depreciation, whilst the company using the annuity method would have charged only £331. The reported profits for these years will reflect this disparity, so before judging a company's performance as good or bad, always study the accounting policies, especially those on depreciation methods adopted.

Depreciation and inflation

During the accountancy profession's experiments with inflation accounting, an attempt was made to substitute each year market values for balance sheet values of fixed assets. These would reflect the rising cost of replacement assets, but would be suitably abated to take their existing years of use into account. The depreciation charge each year would then be calculated afresh on these hypothetical figures. When the collection of so many theoretical market prices was found to be nearly impossible, a similar process was attempted using index numbers measuring inflation, though the well-known Retail Prices Index was found to be too bland for the purpose.

The complexity of such proposals, coupled with the fall in the rate of inflation from over 20% to under 5%, led to their rejection.

Today a simpler method of periodic revaluation of fixed assets is often adopted as a way of trying to make both the balance sheet entries and the cost of depreciation more realistic. This is seldom attempted more often than once every five years, but it will be appreciated that if the book value of a fixed asset is revised upwards but with no extension of its expected remaining life, the annual depreciation charge henceforth must also be revalued upwards.

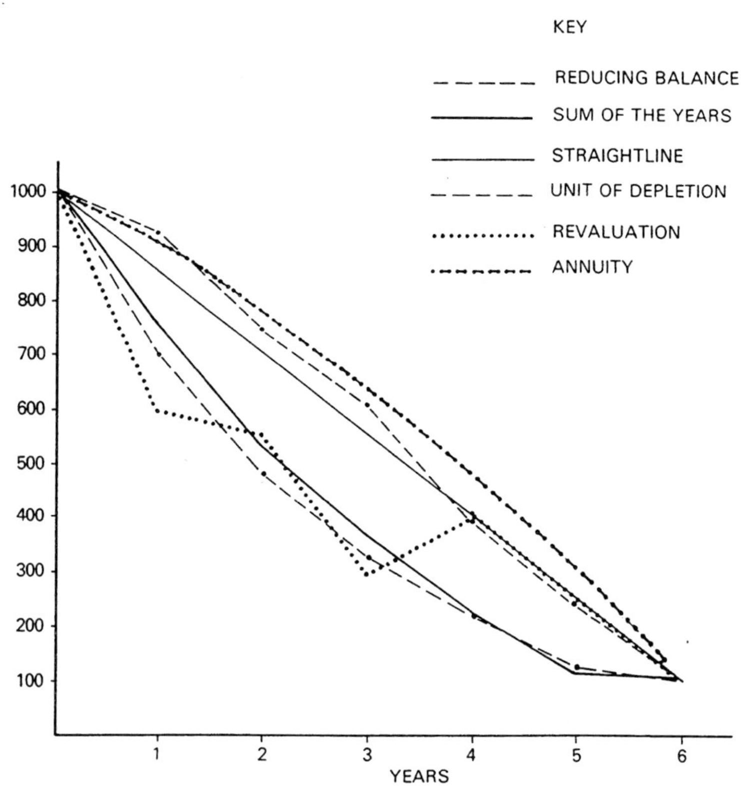

Figure 13. Depreciation methods compared

Revaluing assets upwards certainly improves the appearance of the balance sheet to shareholders, but when they turn the page to see a profit and loss account with a bigger depreciation charge reducing the declared profit for the year, the shareholders must wonder whether revaluations are such a good idea after all.

A final point

Depreciation has one unique feature as an expense. No cash is ever spent on it when it is charged. Thus unlike all the other expenses of the business, from advertising to wages, we never meet such an entry in the cash book. The reason is not hard to find. The cash goes out when the asset is purchased, and therefore in later years there is no further cash expended when the asset is depreciated. It is very important to keep this quirk in mind, for both in the examinations and in practice, most people find it difficult to appreciate that one entry in a profit and loss account never has a corresponding entry in the cash book.

6 Fixed and variable costs

Costing – or cost accounting as it is sometimes called – is a specialised area of accounting, in which instead of recording expenses and income in chronological form, or by category, one relates the expenses to a particular activity. That activity may be the production of motor cars, the processing of chemicals, or the supply of a service such as passenger transport or electricity generation. In short, costing is the way we find out the cost of an activity: it involves bringing together both the expenditure and measured units of output.

As a specialised subject, it has its own literature, and it is as deep a topic as one wishes to make it. All that is considered appropriate for a general introduction is to make one important point which is fundamental to all aspects of costing: this is the distinction between fixed and variable costs.

Fixed costs

Some expenses of a business do not vary with the level of activity, for example, the rent and rates of the premises, the interest payable on a mortgage, the hire or leasing costs of specialised equipment. Such expenses have to be met whether the business is merely 'ticking over' or is operating at maximum capacity. If we are to run a business we must have premises, and no landlord thinks in terms of giving the tenant a discount just because the tenant only uses the premises for some mornings. Another fixed expense is depreciation. Motor cars, in common with most plant, depreciate more in relation to time than to use: the small premium sought for low mileage second-hand cars is the only indication that use is in some way associated with value.

Fixed costs are therefore the minimum cost of being in business. The simplest business must have premises, at least one proprietor or member of staff working, and some fixed assets to depreciate (even if those assets amount to little more than a shelf on which to put the goods being sold and scales with which to weigh them).

Fixed costs are so named because they are fixed in relation to output, but that statement must be subject to some limitation. If a business is successful, it may find that its premises are the limiting factor, because it cannot accommodate any more customers or stock. In such a case, the obvious solution is to take larger premises, and those next door may be ideal. There are few High Streets in the land which have not seen at least one of the big chain stores take over the adjoining premises to enable its trade to be increased. Such an event obviously increases at a stroke the fixed costs of that business.

Costs are therefore only fixed in relation to a certain band of activity. When an increase in productive capacity is needed, it may be necessary to make a bold decision to take on another whole block of fixed expenses. If one delivery lorry cannot cope, the only practical step may be to acquire a second lorry and a second driver, or replace the original lorry with a larger one. Either way, the fixed costs associated with transport are going to be increased substantially.

Variable costs

If fixed costs are those which do not increase in direct proportion to output, it is fairly obvious that variable costs must be those that do. They will include the cost of the goods sold, the power costs of the factory, the labour costs, the telephone and postage costs, all of which can be expected to increase in proportion to output.

In some cases we find semi-variable costs, where there is both an element of fixed and of variable costs. The telephone service is an example. We pay a fixed rental for each exchange line but the charges for the calls are variable costs, depending on their length and number.

It is convenient to think of variable costs as being directly proportional to output, e.g. if we double the number of clothes we make we will double the quantity of material we need, but in practice the cost may not double as other factors such as bulk discounts tend to creep in. On the other hand, if the material required is in short supply we may have to spend more than double to obtain the quantity we need. These aspects can be disregarded at this early stage. What is important to appreciate is that expenses fall into one of the two broad categories: fixed, which do not increase within certain limits of activity; and variable, which can be considered as directly proportional to output.

Break-even charts

The practical consequences of the foregoing is that we can establish what level of activity a business must have if it is to cover all its costs. Clearly, no business can prosper if it has only a trivial amount of activity. Equally obviously, if a business is operating to capacity it should be showing a profit. Somewhere between these two extremes must lie a level of activity at which the income equates with the total expenses. At this level, the business makes neither profit nor loss. We call this the break-even point.

Example

Let us suppose that a small restaurant spends £200 a week on its rent, rates, power and lighting costs. These premises expenses are fixed costs which must be met whether the restaurant is open or closed. It has the minimum staff, a cook and a waitress, whose wages come to £400 a week. The total fixed costs are therefore £600 per week. If the average cost of the food served to each customer is £2, and the average menu charge to customers is £4, what number of customers per week will be needed to achieve break-even?

Figure 14 shows the answer in chart form. The fixed costs of £600 per week give the band across the bottom of the chart. On top of this band, we place the variable costs to give a line of total costs. With no customers, there are no variable costs so the total costs are merely the fixed costs. With 100 customers, the variable costs are

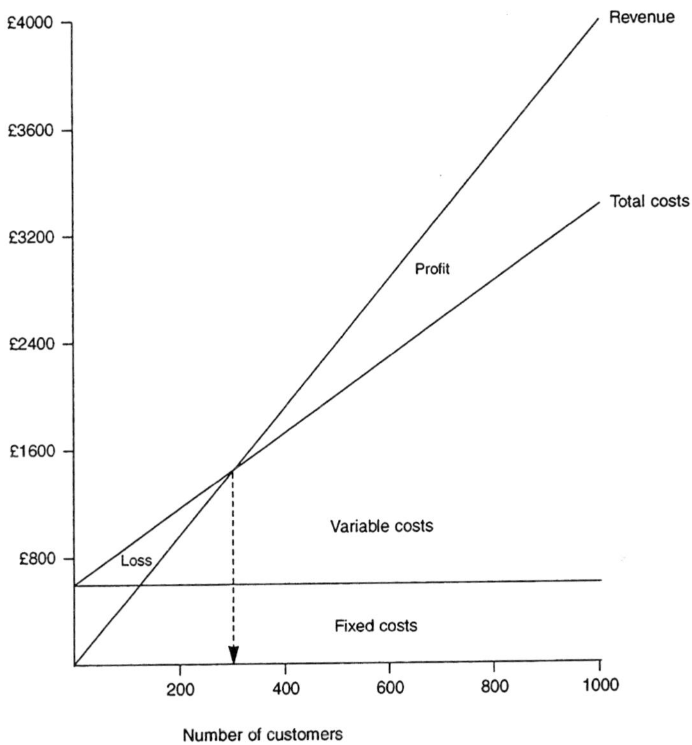

Figure14. A simple break-even chart

£200, making total costs £800. As the variable costs per customer are constant, the line of total costs will be a straight line.

The income of the restaurant with no customers is nil, so the line of revenue must obviously go through the bottom left hand corner. With 100 customers, it will be £400. Again, as the selling price is constant, the line of revenue will be a straight line.

Where the line of revenue crosses the line of total cost, that is the point of break-even. Above that point a profit will be made, below that point a loss is sustained.

It is not difficult to verify the break-even point as 300 customers. The revenue will be £4 x 300 = £1,200. The total costs will be £2 x

300 = £600 for variable costs, plus £600 for fixed costs, making total costs £1,200. If the price to the customers was raised to £5, you should be able to work out the new and lower break-even point.

Contribution

Although graphical presentation is useful by way of example, accountants in practice do not use much graph paper. Instead they use the concept of 'contribution'. Quite simply, this means that if we deduct from the selling price of a unit sale the variable costs, one is left with a figure which is a contribution towards the fixed costs. In Figure 14, the contribution is £2 (£4 selling price, less £2 variable costs). To determine the break-even point, one then divides the fixed costs (£600) by the contribution (£2) to give the break-even point as 300.

When the total contribution on all sales exceeds the fixed costs, the business makes a profit.

Remember that the figure of break-even relates to the period for which we take the fixed costs. In Figure 14, we measured the fixed costs per week, so the break-even point was declared in terms of customers per week. (We could have chosen any other period of time, of course.)

Practical applications

The concept of break-even is extremely important throughout all business activity. Whether we are proposing running a restaurant, an hotel, a bus service, or even putting together an educational course for students, we can identify some expenses as being fixed and some as being variable. No one is going to complain if a profit is made as a result of this activity, but making a loss is a quick way of losing capital and going out of business. It is, therefore, important that in fixing the price we will charge for our service, we see (even if it is a guess) the effect on total costs. A basic understanding of the theories of supply and demand in economics will enable us to understand that the lower the price we charge, the greater will be the demand, and vice versa. It is therefore helpful to know that, in the case of the restaurant, we can achieve break-even with either

300 customers at £4 or 200 customers at £5. (Did you get that calculation right?)

The relative proportions of fixed and variable costs within the total costs of a business will vary depending upon the nature of the business. In the case of the hotel, for instance, the vast majority of the costs will be fixed costs, for the hotel must be rented, equipped and staffed even if nobody arrives to spend the night there. At the other end of the scale, a street trader selling fruit off a barrow will barely have any fixed costs (save his hawker's licence and depreciation on his barrow) but his variable costs will be the cost of the fruit he buys.

In practice, it is hard to estimate expenses with absolute precision. When will postage rates be increased by the Post Office? When will the staff expect a pay rise, and how much? What will next year's business rates be? When can we get a bulk discount on our purchases? Although the expression 'break-even point' is always used, implying some pin point accuracy, we should try to think in terms of a break-even area. Therefore we should think, not of customer No.301 making us a profit, but rather of the fact that if we only get 150 customers we will soon be out of business, whilst if we get 400 regularly we could think about buying the shop next door for expansion.

There are no simple rules about making a profit. Some businesses fix prices high to give a large contribution, and thus need relatively few customers. Other businesses (notably supermarkets) fix prices low, thereby getting a small contribution on each sale but compensating for this by getting vast numbers of sales. In practice, it is often only by experiment and experience that the owner of a business can find out which mixture works best.

Increasing fixed costs

In Figure 14 the fixed costs were shown as a straight line, i.e. they did not vary irrespective of the number of customers. What would be the position if, at an operating level of 400 customers a week, the proprietor considered buying the shop next door? To keep matters simple, let us suppose that the effect would be to double the total fixed costs, on the basis that he had to double the staff as well as the

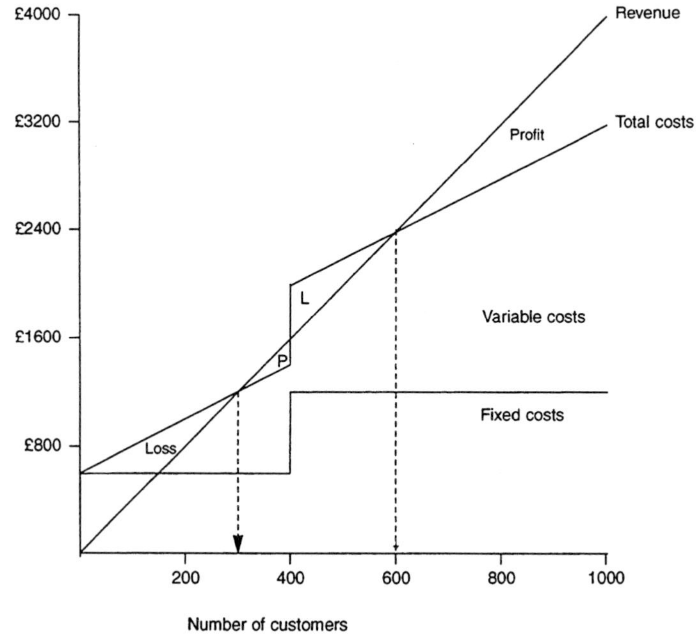

Figure 15. A more complex break-even chart

floor space. There would now be a step in the line of fixed costs, which would rise to £1,200 per week when the number of customers exceeded 400. This step would also take effect in the line of total costs, since although the variable costs did not change from the £2 per customer, the line of total costs would be lifted by the change in the fixed costs.

We can now see two break-even points. The original one still exists at 300 customers per week if he contents himself with the single shop, but although there is a small profit (marked 'P') when custom is between 300 and 400, taking on the extra shop and staff immediately create a loss again (marked 'L') until the turnover gets past the new break-even point of 600 customers.

Most businessmen tend to think that the bigger the business, the bigger the profit. This is too simplistic, for as Figure 15 shows, expansion which involves taking on more fixed expenses can change a profit back into a loss until the business has achieved a considerable expansion to get it past its new break-even point.

This is by no means the end of the story of break-even charts, for we have only considered those with straight lines. In practice we should often be plotting curved lines, showing the effect of bulk discounts for increasing purchases, albeit there may come a curve showing increasing costs when the business becomes so large that all the profit is lost in paying premium rates for supplies and fixed costs that have got out of control by increasing bureaucracy. It is sometimes suggested that the classic portrayal of a business would show two break-even points – one when it grew big enough to get revenue on top of total costs, and the other when it was so large that decreasing amounts of extra revenue at the margin were insufficient to meet the costs of bureaucracy. It is a nice theory and one can make some interesting cases, such as where a railway company might duplicate tracks to enable more trains to carry more passengers, but it is unlikely any but a very few businesses would grow to the size where expansion resulted in the profits being lost in fresh costs.

7 Cash flow forecasts

It is fundamental in every business that there must be planning, and one of the most important areas for such planning is cash flow. It is one of the hard lessons you learn in life that when you run out of money, you run out of friends. In business, if you cannot pay your suppliers they will stop selling you goods on credit and revert to a cash-with-order basis of trading. If you cannot pay the landlord his rent, he will demand the key of the door back. And if you cannot pay your staff on pay day, they will not come to work the next day – though they may turn up to ask for their P.45 tax form!

Blind faith that somehow the income will enable the outgoings to be met is not enough: as good crystal balls with fortune telling capabilities are not easy to come by, one has to resort to science to predict the future. We do this with cash flow forecasts.

A cash flow forecast is not difficult to prepare once one has all the details available, but getting those details may well prove extremely difficult. Traditionally, one prepares these statements for 12 months ahead, though certain businesses working on a weekly cycle might make them for 52 weeks. Trying to look more than a year ahead is inviting blind guesses to take the place of calculated forecasts. To prepare a statement for less than a year is being a little short-sighted, though, for example, it might help a society mid-year to see if and how they might get to the end of the financial year, when the influx of annual subscriptions will again make it solvent.

An important thing to remember with a cash flow forecast is that it is no more than that – a forecast of cash flow. Therefore, like weather forecasts, we must accept it is unlikely to be 100% accurate. We must also recognise that in forecasting cash flow we are not necessarily forecasting profit, and certainly the words 'profit' and 'loss' will not appear within it. Nor will the charge for depreciation, since as pointed out earlier, the cash goes out when we buy the fixed assets, not when we depreciate them.

Today, cash flow forecasting is regarded as so important by lending bank managers that it will be a very lucky (or trusted!) businessman who seeks a material overdraft and is not asked for such a document. Worse still, bankers have forms on which to record not only the forecast figures of cash flow monthly but also an adjacent column in which to insert the actual figure with the benefit of hindsight. (Mercifully, the second columns seldom seem to get filled!)

It must be appreciated that any cash flow forecast (or 'cash budget' as some people prefer to call them) is a welding together of a great many plans, estimates and assumptions. If one can achieve a result in practice which is within 10% or 15% of one's prediction (say a bank balance at the year end of £23,000 – £17,000, against a forecast of £20,000, it is good forecasting. Few businessmen regard all income and expenses as being under complete control, for although inflation may be modest it is never constant for long and so all prices are liable to change. Similarly, although one may give customers a month's credit, what is the likelihood that all will pay on the due date? And will some go bankrupt and never pay?

Bankers like to see cash flow forecasts for two reasons: in the first place, they may enable the lending banker to see when (and if) he will get repayment of the requested loan; secondly, the mere production of such a document is a good indication that the customer has given a great deal of forethought to all the financial aspects of the business, to be followed, hopefully, by a measure of self-discipline in trying to achieve the forecast result. In a business which buys and sells goods on credit, for example, the following factors will all affect cash flow and must therefore be taken into the reckoning in preparing a cash flow forecast.

The following list is by no means exhaustive, but indicates how much work can be involved in dealing with what appeared to be a simple request from the banker about 'How will cash run next year?'

Once you have all the information, writing out a cash flow

INFLOW

Any addition to capital, with date and amount;

Sales:

- prices generally;
- trade or bulk discounts;
- overall level;
- monthly fluctuations;
- period of credit taken by customers;
- incidence of bad debts;

Any other income (e.g. interest, commission);

Any disposal of fixed assets.

OUTFLOW

Any withdrawal of capital or dividends, with date and amount;

Purchases:

- prices generally;
- trade or bulk discounts;
- relation to sales budget (e.g. is stockholding going to match sales, reduce or increase?)
- monthly fluctuations;
- period of credit obtainable from suppliers;

Expenses:

- their nature, timing and credit period;

Fixed assets:

- identity of any fixed assets to be acquired, with date, amount and method of financing (e.g. cash, hire purchase, finance lease);

Staff costs:

- identities, salary scales, fringe benefits or costs;
- increase or reduction in staffing;

Drawings:

- dates and amounts;

Tax payments:

- dates and amounts.

---

forecast is simple. We take a sheet of paper with 12 columns and head these columns with the names of the forthcoming months. The forecast is usually prepared for the accounting year, so although the illustrations given below run from January to December, bear in mind that if your accounting date is 30 April, the columns would run from May through to April.

At the top of the sheet we set out in the appropriate column all the cash we expect to receive from any source. It does not matter whether it is normal income, e.g. sales, or a non-recurring source such as the disposal of a fixed asset: if it is money coming in, it must be recorded.

Similarly with the money we expect to pay out, regardless of whether we are paying for purchases, expenses, fixed assets or withdrawing money for personal use, i.e. drawings, this money is recorded.

Having totalled both sections, we deduct the total payments each month from the total receipts to arrive at a figure we call 'net for the month'. All that is left to be done then is to add this to the opening cash balance for that month and arrive at a closing balance for the month, which is then in turn carried forward as the opening balance of the next month. The bottom line is therefore the expected cash or bank balance at the end of each month.

Some months we must expect to find that the payments exceed the receipts. It is tempting then to put a minus sign against the figure, but it is better not to, as minus signs tends to get confused with the dashes we may use when there is a box left empty. Some people then reach for a red pen, but again this is not recommended: cash flow forecasts are often photocopied for the banker or other interested person, and the vast majority of photocopiers will turn red figures into black figures! The universal convention when one meets minus figures in accountancy is to put the figures inside brackets.

A simple example shows the arrangement.

I have a salary of £1,000 per month after tax. My birthday is in April and I have an aunt who invariably sends me a cheque for £200 as a birthday present. I put aside £400 a month for housekeeping and I pay £80 per month rent. My electricity bills arrive in January, April, July and October and I pay them the following month: they are usually about £100 each quarter. In June I expect to buy a car for £850: in the same month I shall have to pay £350 for the annual licence and insurance on it and in that month and each following month I expect to spend about £60 for running expenses.

Every month I also expect to spend about £200 on personal expenses, such as clothes, entertainment and magazines. I pay £50 each month on a life assurance policy. My bank balance on 1 January is £200. What will my bank balance be on 31 December?

The cash flow forecast is set out below.

	Jan	Feb	Mar	Apr	May	Jun	Jul	Aug	Sep	Oct	Nov	Dec
RECEIPTS												
Salary	1000	1000	1000	1000	1000	1000	1000	1000	1000	1000	1000	1000
Birthday present				200								
	1000	1000	1000	1200	1000	1000	1000	1000	1000	1000	1000	1000
PAYMENTS												
Housekeeping	400	400	400	400	400	400	400	400	400	400	400	400
Rent	80	80	80	80	80	80	80	80	80	80	80	80
Electricity		100			100			100			100	
Purchase of car						850						
Licence and insurance						350						
Running expenses						60	60	60	60	60	60	60
Personal expenses	200	200	200	200	200	200	200	200	200	200	200	200
Life insurance	50	50	50	50	50	50	50	50	50	50	50	50
	730	830	730	730	830	1990	790	890	790	790	890	790
NET FOR MONTH	270	170	270	470	170	(990)	210	110	210	210	110	210
BALANCE B/FWD	200	470	640	910	1380	1550	560	770	880	1090	1300	1410
BALANCE C/FWD	470	640	910	1380	1550	560	770	880	1090	1300	1410	1620

Figure 16. Cash flow forecast

My bank balance at the end of December will be £1,620 if all my predictions work out precisely. In practice, like the weather forecast, there will be some variations and these always seem to involve more expenditure (e.g. repairs to the car) or a reduction in income (e.g. salary remaining constant but tax deductions increasing). In the above example, neither of these would be very serious as there is a comfortable bank balance throughout the year, as shown by the figures in the bottom row. Often, however, when preparing cash flow forecasts for abusiness we would add an extra line and call it 'Contingencies'. For the above example, we might make it an extra payment of £50 per month.

Frequently in business situations the bottom row will include some figures in brackets indicating that an overdraft will be required if the expenditure is to be met as forecast. In this case, instead of adding in a line for contingencies we may look at the forecast overdraft and, to use an old banking expression, 'put a bit of elastic in it'. Thus if the biggest forecast overdraft was shown as £1,527, we would seek an overdraft limit of £2,000.

In dealing with overdrawn positions, we must recognise that interest will be payable, but unless the amounts involved are substantial it is unnecessary to calculate these: the 'elastic' in our forecast is often sufficient to cover them. In other cases, the forecast overdraft limit is so unrealistic that it would be a waste of effort to make such calculations and we must try and rearrange the cash flow forecast to more reasonable plans. A further example will show this process.

Arthur is starting a publishing business on 1 January with £5,000 in his bank account. That month he will buy office furniture for £700, paying by cheque, and will also rent a small office for £400 per month, such rent including lighting, heating, rates and cleaning charges. In February he will commission a book from an author and pay him £1,000 advance royalty. He undertakes to pay a further £1,000 when he receives the text: this is scheduled for May.

Arthur will place the book for typesetting in June. This will cost £1,000 which he will have to pay in August. In June, Arthur will make a contract with a printer. He expects the printer to require an immediate payment of £1,400 to cover the cost of the paper needed, with the balance of the printing cost, £1,800, being payable in November when he will also have to pay the binding cost of £900.

Arthur will be obtaining a grant of £2,000 towards the costs from a sponsoring body and he expects to receive this in August. He estimates that he will be able to get some advance orders from booksellers on a cash-with-order basis of the following amounts: September £750; October £1,300; November £2,100.

In November, when he receives stocks of the book from the binder, he forecasts that he will be sending out books with invoices totalling a further £5,000. In December his estimate of further despatches with invoices is £7,000. In both these cases, he will allow the booksellers one month's credit.

What overdraft facilities will he need to see this programme through and what will his bank balance be at 31 December?

As you may wish to practice your newly acquired skills in drawing up cash flow forecasts, the answer is shown overleaf.

There are several points to note when you have completed your forecast and compared it to the model answer shown on the next page in Figure 17.

The first is that the invoices totalling £7,000 sent out to booksellers in December will not be expected to produce any cash until January, since they are being given one month's credit. Accordingly, this cash will not be shown in this year's forecast, but will appear in that for the following year.

The second point is that an overdraft facility (say, with elastic, of £2,500) starting in June, will be required, but this is expected to be fully repaid in December. It may seem surprising that no provision for interest is made, but even taking a simplistic view of this at 1% per month on the closing balance, the total interest would only be of the order of £67, which is not material in the context of the figures.

Clearly Arthur must have other income than that expected from the publishing business, since no provision for drawings has been made.

Remember that cash flow forecasts are no more than that. Thus we cannot expect to see any figure of profit or loss from this statement, though it is not difficult to deduce that a profit is being made by the publishing business, since the £7,000 debtors (unpaid invoices to booksellers) at 31 December when coupled to the closing bank balance of £3,550 is clearly more than his opening capital of £5,000 and there appear to be no outstanding liabilities.

We frequently find that we need to draft several cash flow forecasts for the same business before we get one which is acceptable to all concerned. Suppose in this case the banker declines to make any overdraft facilities available? Does Arthur point to the fact that his forecast shows a comfortable credit balance by the end of his first year's trading? The banker may well demand some form of security which Arthur cannot supply. Now what happens?

Arthur must modify his plan and there are several ways he can do this. He could persuade the author, perhaps, to wait for his

	Jan	Feb	Mar	Apr	May	Jun	Jul	Aug	Sep	Oct	Nov	Dec
RECEIPTS												
Grant								2000				
Advance orders									750	1300	2100	
Booksellers												5000
								2000	750	1300	2100	5000
PAYMENTS												
Office furniture	700											
Rent	400	400	400	400	400	400	400	400	400	400	400	400
Author		1000			1000							
Typesetting								1000				
Printer						1400					1800	
Binding											900	
	1100	1400	400	400	1400	1800	400	1400	400	400	3100	400
NET FOR MONTH	(1100)	(1400)	(400)	(400)	(1400)	(1800)	(400)	600	350	900	(1000)	4600
BALANCE B/FWD	5000	3900	2500	2100	1700	300	(1500)	(1900)	(1300)	(950)	(50)	(1050)
BALANCE C/FWD	3900	2500	2100	1700	300	(1500)	(1900)	(1300)	(950)	(50)	(1050)	3550

Figure 17. Cash flow forecast for Arthur

fee until the end of the year. Alternatively, the printer and/or the typesetter might be willing to give a little more credit. With a bigger discount offered for the cash-with-order advance orders, he might get more money from the booksellers earlier, even at the cost of a reduction in his eventual profit. Arthur might use all, or a combination of some of these factors.

Receiving and giving credit is the most common way of massaging cash flow into an acceptable pattern. Few suppliers are willing to give credit to new businesses run by people not previously known to them: the usual response is for the supplier to say 'It's cash and carry for the first six months, and perhaps we'll talk about credit terms at the end of that time'. If a new business gives credit (as with the invoices to booksellers in the case of Arthur), the effect is to delay for at least one month the receipt of money, and to open the door to the possibility of bad debts as well. Although in bygone years even small businesses gave credit or hire purchase facilities, most were only too happy to indicate, when credit cards became widespread, that credit terms were no longer given to anyone.

8 The flow of funds

Every business needs working capital. Working capital is the amount by which current assets (notably stock, debtors and cash) exceed current liabilities (those creditors which fall due for payment within the next year, including not only trade creditors, accrued expenses, and taxation, but also any bank overdraft). The reason for including bank overdrafts as a current liability may seem curious, since in many businesses it is to be seen in the balance sheet every year, but the legal nicety is that a banker may call in an overdraft instantly, whereas a bank loan is usually granted (like a house mortgage) for a specific period of years.

Working capital is the life blood of the business and it circulates through the entire business activity. Figure 18 illustrates the basic principle. Starting with cash, the business buys supplies of goods and services such as labour to create work in progress. This in turn becomes finished goods from which sales may be made. How long the working capital is tied up in stock depends to a large extent on the nature of the particular trade. Thus, a supermarket expects to turn its stock over in two weeks, but a jeweller must be able to offer a good selection of rings and brooches and he will be lucky to turn his stock over in less than two years. Think of the lost interest on the funds tied up for that time, and you will begin to understand why a jeweller must make a good rate of gross profit on his sales. In many businesses, the sales are made on credit terms which produce debtors, who will hopefully pay their debts to replenish the cash.

The successful business will try to ensure that the cash inflow (mainly from debtors) is as great as, or greater than, the cash outgoing for further supplies. You may think that this is bound to happen if the business is trading at a profit, but unfortunately profit flow is

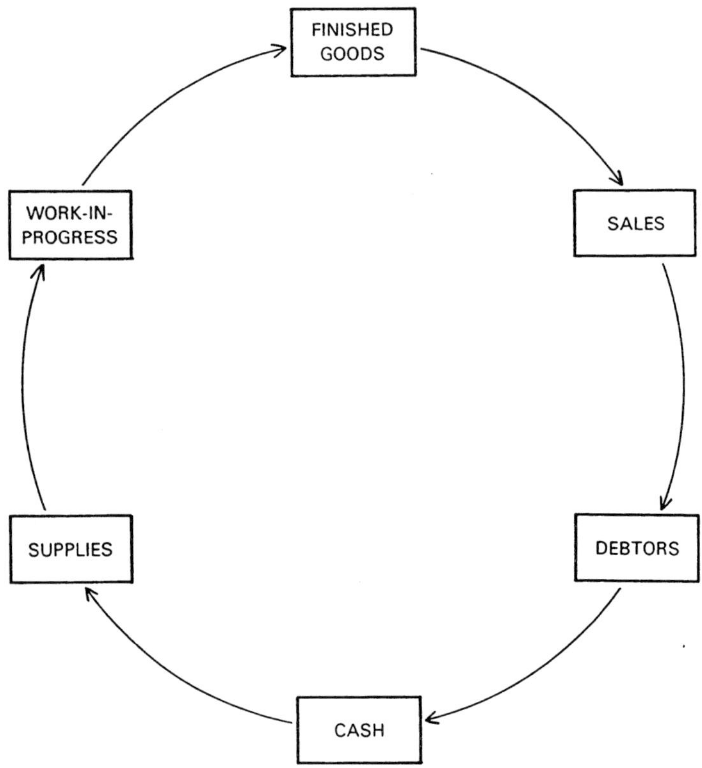

Figure 18. How working capital rotates

not always matched by cash flow, for, as Figure 19 demonstrates, working capital can and does get lost! Some of the available cash must be used for the purchase of fixed assets which will help to earn the profits, whilst theft, errors in production and wastage will also take their toll. Even when finished goods are ready for sale, some are likely to suffer deterioration or obsolescence, whilst again theft is an ever present risk. Although the business may declare a profit when the goods are sold at proper prices, that profit and more can be lost through the incidence of bad debts.

Finally, every business which makes a profit has to pay tax

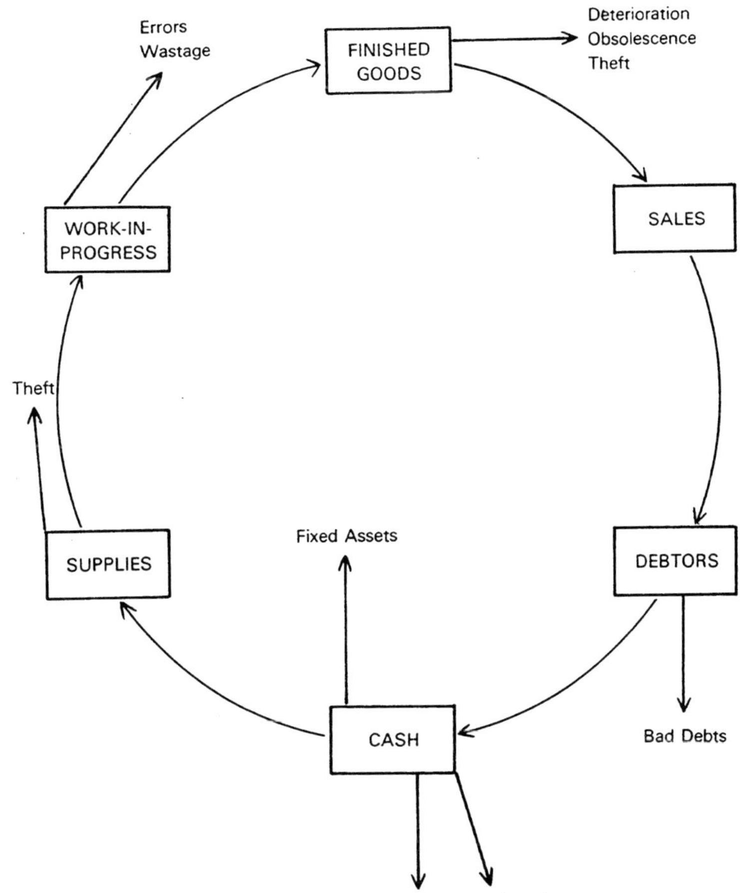

Figure 19. How working capital gets lost.

thereon, and Collectors of Taxes insist on being paid with money. Likewise, shareholders who see their company making a profit will expect to be paid a dividend, which will further deplete the cash resources.

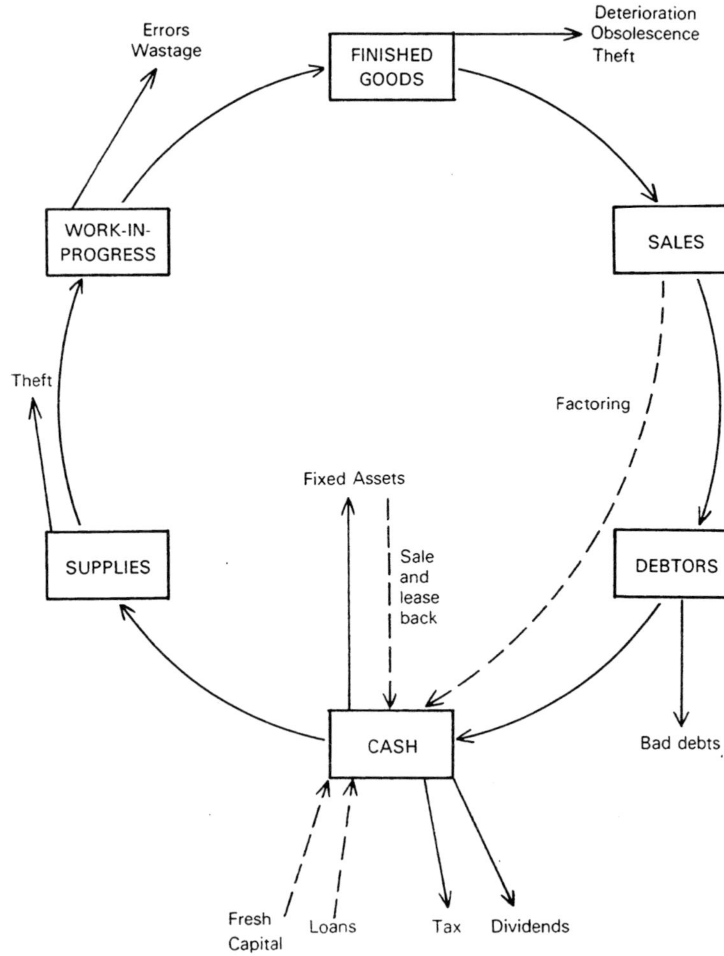

Figure 20. How working capital gets augmented

Put all these factors together, and you get the picture of a central heating system with a great many leaking joints!

The obvious remedy would seem to be to try and stop all the leaks, and certainly every business tries to do just that, by security systems, maintaining stocks at as low a level as is compatible with maintaining adequate variety, and by chasing debtors who do not pay promptly. But there is a limit to what can be done in stopping leaks, and it is therefore necessary to augment the working capital, by the methods shown in Figure 20.

Fixed assets do not have to deplete the working capital, for there are several ways in which they can be acquired with the cost spread over their working life. A building which is owned can be sold (to an insurance company or pension fund) and leased back, thereby releasing the capital tied up. New premises could be taken on a long lease instead of being purchased, and even equipment can be obtained in a similar manner by the use of finance leases, which are effectively a lease for the life of that asset. Possibly a majority of the world's aircraft are held on finance leases, where the capital has been provided by finance companies and the airlines are making monthly payments for the use of the aircraft out of the fares that are received. Finance leases tend to be used for the so-called 'Big Ticket' items (those involving millions of pounds) whilst smaller assets have their cost spread by the use of hire purchase or sales on extended credit.

Many businesses receive immediate payment when they sell goods on credit by the use of factoring arrangements. Under this process, a finance company will provide, say, 75% or 80% of the face value of the sales invoice against an assignment to it of that debt. The balance (less interest charges and other costs) will be paid to the trader when the customer settles their account, but the whole process enables the business to regard their sales as being almost all cash sales, albeit at reduced prices. What happens if the customer does not pay? This depends on the precise terms of the factoring agreement, for in some cases the finance company will return the bad debt to the trader and reclaim the advance made, whilst in other cases the finance company, having charged a little extra for the service, will accept the loss caused by the bad debt.

Growing businesses, like growing children, need feeding: even large public companies will periodically turn to their bankers, their shareholders, or the money market generally to raise further long term capital. Most companies appear to want to continue their growth indefinitely, though a few have actually decided they are big enough and have reduced their capital base by buying back for cancellation some of their share capital. (This ability of a company to purchase its own shares was introduced by the Companies Act 1981 (now consolidated in the Companies Act 1985), but it has only been in the last few years that the stock exchange has seen this process carried out on any scale.)

Shares and loans may appear to be at opposite ends of the financial spectrum: the former gives the holder no promise of any future income but a vote in its affairs, whilst the latter will always have to promise interest payments but deny the holder any voting right. Although this is true in most cases, a popular compromise in recent decades has been the convertible loan. Like the life cycle of the butterfly, this instrument changes its form entirely during a successful life. It starts as loan paying interest, but with the addition of an option to convert it into shares at a predetermined rate during a fixed period. Because investors will usually consider this option to be of value, the convertible loan stock will carry a lower rate of interest than would have to be paid on pure loan stock. If the company prospers, the option to convert into shares when the appropriate time comes will give the holder a capital profit; if the company does not prosper, the holder continues to hold it as loan stock which will then be repaid at par by the company after a fixed period.

A Funds Flow Statement

To demonstrate to shareholders and other interested parties how the funds within a company would change, it became the fashion for companies to supplement their annual accounts with a simple statement showing the changes. A brief example is shown in Figure 21.

A word of explanation on the depreciation is probably required. The annual charge for depreciation is an adjustment of the book value of fixed assets which has not involved any payment of money: the money was paid when the fixed assets were purchased, not when they are depreciated. In measuring the use of funds in the business, therefore, we must add back the depreciation which has been charged, for it will have decreased the profit but has not involved any expenditure in the present year.

Good Traders Ltd
Statement of Source and Application of Funds
Year ended 31 December 19..

	£	£
Sources		
Net profit for the year	34,400	
Add depreciation charged in year	600	35,000
Proceeds of share issue in year		50,000
		85,000
Applications		
Fixed assets purchased	55,000	
Dividends paid	10,000	65,000
Balance, being increase in working capital	20,000	
Increase in stock	22,500	
Decrease in debtors	(5,500)	
Increase in creditors	(3,000)	
Decrease in bank overdraft	6,000	20,000

Figure 21. A funds flow statement

The share capital has clearly added to the company's funds, and this would be stated at the total amount received, including any share premium.

A statement on these lines was made a compulsory appendix to all annual accounts of companies having a turnover of £25,000 or more by SSAP 10 in 1973.

There are fashions in everything, however, and this requirement was rescinded in 1991 when the first of the new Financial Reporting Standards, FRS 1, was issued by the accountancy profession. This declared, in effect, that 'Cash is King' and that there was an urgent need to draw attention to the cash flow rather than the more vague concept of funds. Accordingly, a format was laid down for a Cash Flow Statement to be appended to all published company accounts other than 'small' companies. (The definition of such a company

Notasmall Company Limited
Cash Flow Statement for the year ended 31 December 19..

	£m	£m
Net cash inflow from operating activities		6,889*
Returns on investments and servicing of finance		
Interest received	3,011	
Interest paid	(12)	2,999
Taxation		(2,922)
Capital expenditure		
Payments to acquire intangible fixed assets	(71)	
Payments to acquire tangible fixed assets	(1,496)	
Receipts from sales of tangible fixed assets	42	(1,525)
		5,441
Equity dividends paid		(2,417)
		3,024
Management of liquid resources		
Purchase of treasury bills	(650)	
Sale of treasury bills	200	(450)
Financing		
Issue of ordinary share capital	211	
Repurchase of debenture loan	(149)	
Expenses paid in connection with share issues	(5)	57
Increase in cash		2,631

*A separate statement would show how this resulted from the operating profit, increased by the charge for depreciation and after changes in levels of stocks, debtors and creditors.

Figure 22. A Cash Flow Statement

changes as inflation continues to make big figures look smaller, but currently a 'small' company is one that meets at least two of the following conditions: annual turnover not more than £2.8 million; balance sheet total not more than £1.4 million; average number of employees not more than 50. So a small company can be quite a big company to most people!)

In rescinding the need to publish a Statement of Source and Application of Funds, which had affected most companies, FRS 1 has therefore made the Cash Flow Statement an obligation for only a minority of all companies. FRS 1 was itself revised in 1996, and a simple example of such a Cash Flow Statement is shown in Figure 22.

9 Accounting ratios

There is always an attraction for simple figures. How much easier it is to comprehend that 30% of sales proceeds were profit, rather than be told that total sales amounted to £812,526 and the profit was £243,757. And the bigger the figures get, the easier it is to get dazzled by them – few people other than statisticians and perhaps politicians can really say they understand what a million or more is.

By calling these simple figures 'ratios' you might expect to find them in just that format, e.g. 150 is to 300 as 1 is to 2 (or 150:300::1:2 in statistical notation). In fact, the figures sometimes do get used in that format, but more often we use the information in percentage form, e.g. net profit is 9.8% of sales. Pocket calculators make percentages very easy to calculate, but we have to be careful to curb the obsessive detail of the calculator which presents us with a figure of 9.7523678%: one place of decimals, rounded if necessary, is usually quite sufficient otherwise the 'simple' presentation may well have more digits to consider than the original data.

Accounting ratios can also come in decimal form (e.g. 15% presented as 0.15) or even as fractions (25% presented as 1/4). Each accountant or manager tends to have his own preference in these matters and all are acceptable. (When a chief examiner for an accountancy paper changes, you may also find a different format being used.)

The following table shows some percentages presented in the format of ratios or fractions. If you would like to practice your skills in making such translations, cover the middle and right hand columns with a sheet of paper and make your own calculations.

Some loss of fine detail is obviously going to take place as we round off to whole numbers (or one or two places of decimals) but

Percentage	Ratio	Fraction
10	1:10	1/10
25	1:4	1/4
50	1:2	1/2
80	4:5	4/5
14	1:7	1/7
33	1:3	1/3
1	1:100	1/100
75	3:4	3/4
63	5:8 (or 1:1.6)	5/8

this is allowable since we still have the precise data available if we need it, but comprehension is so much easier when we keep figures simple. The second place of decimals in a percentage is seldom necessary – the difference between 43.8% and 43.81% is one part in ten thousandths, and is that really meaningful?

The Logic of Accounting Ratios

In studying the examples which follow, what must be borne in mind is that there is clearly some relationship between the two figures being brought together, i.e. the numerator and denominator of the fraction.

Accounting Ratios is not merely an exercise in mathematics. Obviously it would be of no consequence to arrive at a conclusion that Company A always makes a profit at least ten times as large as its telephone number, whilst the profit of Company B is only three times its telephone number! No one but a mathematician (and perhaps a demented one at that) would even start to look for an association between profit and telephone numbers. But we would expect to find a relationship (or positive correlation, as the statisticians term it) between the size of a company's turnover and its profit. Bigger turnover should result in bigger profit.

Accounts for Ratios plc
Profit and loss account
Year ended 31 December ....

Turnover		X	**A**
Less Cost of sales:			
Stock 1st January	X		
Add Purchases in year	X		**B**
	X		
Less Stock 31st December	X	X	**C**
Gross profit		X	**D**
Administrative expenses		X	
		X	
Interest paid		X	**E**
Net profit before taxation		X	**F**
Taxation		X	
Net profit after tax		X	**G**
Dividends paid and proposed		X	**H**
Retained profits for the year		X	

Accounts for Ratios plc
Balance sheet – 31 December ....

Fixed assets		X	**I**
Current assets			
Stock	X		**J**
Debtors	X		**K**
Cash	X		**L**
	X		**M**
Creditors: amounts falling due within one year			
Trade creditors	X		**N**
Accrued expenses	X		
Bank overdraft	X		
	X		**P**
Net current assets		X	
Total assets less current liabilities		X	
Creditors: amounts falling due after more than one year			
Debentures		X	**Q**
		X	
Share capital and reserves			
Called up share capital	X		**R**
General reserve	X		
Profit and loss account	X	X	**S**

Figure 23. Accounting ratios

It is always vital to keep the logic of a relationship in mind. Examiners are not above trying to tempt one into nonsense areas, e.g. by drawing attention to the fact that whereas stock was equal to twice the amount of the bank overdraft last year, in the present year it is three times that sum. No doubt some candidates will fall for the bait and dutifully write 'It is a good (or poor, or dangerous, or cautious) feature that the growth in the stock has overtaken the growth in the bank overdraft' – and incur five penalty marks for nonsense! Figures of stock and bank overdraft have nothing in common. The increase in the bank overdraft may have been caused by the purchase of fixed assets, or the prompt payment of creditors to obtain cash discounts – in short, almost everything will affect it. So why blame it all on stock?

Accounting Ratios are a form of financial shorthand – be careful that yours do not become mere scribbles!

In the following examples, the bold letters **A** to **S** have been added to enable you to see where the ingredients have been shown in the example of annual accounts on Figure 23.

Gross Profit Percentage

Gross profit/Turnover x 100 **(D/A)**

Gross profit is the excess of sales proceeds over the cost of the goods sold. This ratio is the most important of all ratios used by accountants: gross profit is the fund from which all the expenses of the business are paid, and hopefully some will be left over to share with the Inland Revenue as tax, and the shareholders as dividend.

The level of gross profit will vary with the particular trade and also with the position of the business in that trade. Thus in catering, a transport cafe may live happily with a gross profit of only 25%, whilst a city centre restaurant will expect to see more than 50% in many cases. The reason for this apparent disparity is that the level of rent and furnishings in a transport cafe will usually be quite low, whilst a city centre restaurant will have a more sophisticated and hence more costly environment. Some supermarkets may exist on a mere 10% gross profit (relying on the vast turnover to generate a sufficient amount to cover all expenses), whilst the 'shop on the corner' which is open all hours will be charging materially more for the same goods to give it a gross profit percentage at least double that needed by the supermarket.

In this, as with all ratios, there is no percentage which is right or wrong. Every business makes its own decision where to place itself in marketing terms, and a strategy that works for one business may be fatal for another. Within the first year of the life of a business, the management will address these problems of pricing and arrive at a pattern which works – or go out of business! What is of value in studying accounting ratios is not the figure per se but the comparison with the previous year. 'Why are we making only 18% gross profit when we made 22% last year?' is the question a trader may ask himself. Finding the answer to that is sometimes a challenge. It may be because the customers or the staff are stealing the stock. Or it may be that a large volume of stock was lost in an accident or a fire and not covered by insurance. Or it may simply be that the trader has deliberately lowered his selling prices in a bid to make more profit, for by reducing his profit on each individual sale he may make many more sales which more than compensate.

Finding the reasons why accounting ratios have varied is where skill is needed, and it may be necessary to make detailed investigations to find the answer. What, at first sight, may appear worrying (a lower gross profit percentage) may prove to be quite acceptable when it arises from a change of policy in pricing which has doubled total turnover.

It is always necessary to keep a sense of proportion and not tell an examiner 'It is a sign of great weakness that in the current year the gross profit percentage has dropped from 37.6% to 37.5%'. Accounting ratios in any business will always wobble – in fact if they were identical each year an auditor could be very suspicious, recognising that the figures had been 'manufactured' for his benefit and did not arise from true records. If you were driving a car behind a cyclist, you would expect the cyclist to wobble a little, and you make due allowance for that fact. So a gross profit varying plus-or-minus 0.5% would be interpreted as a normal wobble. But a gross profit that shrank to only two-thirds would not be a wobble but a very dangerous swerve! Distinguishing between the acceptable wobbles and the unacceptable swerves is a skill which will only come with practice and experience.

Falling gross profit is always a change to be taken seriously. Inspectors of Taxes often make their own judgments on sole traders when they see this feature – they are prone to take it as evidence that some of the sales receipts have been put into the trader's pocket instead of the till!

Net Profit Percentage

Net profit/Turnover x 100 **(F/A)**

Net profit expressed as a percentage of sales will seldom have the same expected consistency each year as the gross profit, for net profit is what is left when all other expenses have been charged. An expensive roof repair, a strike by staff, an unsuccessful advertising campaign will all have their effect on the final figure of profit. Few businesses make even 10% net profit on sales, but comparisons of the percentage with previous years will often disclose welcome or unwelcome trends.

Return on Shareholders' Funds

Net profit before tax/Shareholders' funds x 100 **(F/S)**

The object of shareholders subscribing money to a company is that it will make profits. The more money is subscribed for shares, the greater the profits which will arise. At least, that is the theory and the expectation. To enable a comparison to be made with what might be achieved in other investments (e.g. bank or building society accounts), it is useful to express the net profit made in any year with the total funds which the shareholders have in the business. We divide the net profit (before tax) by the total of share capital and reserves. We are obviously not concerned merely with the money originally subscribed by the shareholders, but also further investment which has arisen through profits having been made in earlier periods and not paid out as dividend. The total funds of shareholders are often referred to as the 'equity funds'.

In making comparisons of this percentage with other yields being offered (e.g. market rates of interest), we must be careful to realise that with all accounting ratios, we will get only as much accuracy out of the calculation as we put into it. If the fixed assets of the business are undervalued (e.g. freehold property bought years ago and not revalued), then the funds of the shareholders will also be understated. Some fixed assets such as goodwill, trade marks and patents may have been completely written off. Obviously if we divide a figure of this year's net profit by a figure for funds which may be only half the realistic present market value, the percentage emerging will appear as double what it should be.

This ratio is a useful test of whether or not the shareholders' funds are being soundly used, but it is subject to this major restriction that fixed assets must be realistically valued.

Return on Total Funds Employed

Net profit before tax + Debenture interest/Shareholders' funds + Debentures
(F + E/S + Q)

In addition to the funds of shareholders in a company, there is often money borrowed long-term, referred to as being the 'loan capital'. It may take a form of debentures (as suggested in the above notation) or it may be a mortgage on a property, a bank loan, loan notes, or a combination of these.

The total funds employed in the business are therefore a combination of the shareholders' funds and the loan capital. Since the loan capital will incur an interest charge each year, we must add back this figure to the net profit if we are to make a meaningful calculation of how much the business is earning as a return on its total funds employed.

This is where the subject of 'gearing' comes in (explained later in this chapter). If a company can earn on its total funds employed a return greater than that which it has to pay in interest charges on the loan capital, it is beneficial to the shareholders to have loan capital in the company. For example, if the company earns 12% on the funds it employs and can borrow at only 10%, the extra 2% means a little more profit for the shareholders.

The danger with gearing, of course, is that, although the shareholders may not complain too much if a bad year means that they do not get a dividend, it is of no consequence to the lenders of funds whether the company makes a profit or a loss: loan and mortgage interest is payable regardless of the consequences to the paying company.

The same caution applies about the realistic valuation of fixed assets if the percentages calculated are to be compared to the market rates. Even ignoring this point, if the Return of Total Funds Employed is less than the Return on Shareholders' Funds, it is an indication that borrowing loan capital has been a success, as some of the return on the loan capital has not gone to the lenders but has 'spilt over' to the benefit of the shareholders.

Earnings per Share
Net profit after tax/Number of shares in issue
(G/Number of shares issued)

The stock market uses the concept of earnings per share as the primary measure of performance of a listed company. This is determined by taking the net profit after tax for an accounting year and dividing it by the number of ordinary shares in issue and ranking for dividend for that year. The figure is published as a number of pence per share, the number being taken to one place of decimals, e.g. 22.7p.

The calculation is made on the basis of SSAP 3, which was published in 1974. The rules for calculation take into account all possible changes which may affect a company's share capital including capitalisation (or bonus) issues and the conversion of certain loan stock into shares. As a result of such comprehensive rules it is always safe to say that an increase in the earnings per share (EPS) is good news for shareholders, and a decrease is always bad news. In other words, you can judge by the figure and ignore the chairman's excuses why it is down on the previous year!

The EPS is calculated once a year on the basis of the audited accounts, and although not part of the profit and loss account it is published at the foot of that document, with the detailed calculations usually shown in the accompanying notes.

In recent years, listed companies have taken to calculating EPS figures on the abbreviated half-year accounts they publish, but SSAP 3 does not require this extra publication, and it should be remembered that the half-yearly figures (which the Stock Exchange insists are published by listed companies) are not subjected to audit. EPS calculations are only made for listed companies, for such companies do not receive any gifts from the commercial world and they pay for all goods and services received. By contrast, private companies may have the benefit of interest-free loans from directors, and even the use of premises owned by directors which are not the subject of market rents. It is therefore considered that EPS calculations for private companies would not necessarily be meaningful.

Price/Earnings Ratio
Market price of share/EPS

The stock market finds a second use for the EPS figure. By dividing it into the daily closing price of a listed share, it arrives at a Price/Earnings Ratio, usually abbreviated to P/E or pe. This will be calculated afresh each night and quality newspapers publish it against the price of the share, together with the EPS.

This figure is not a percentage or a money figure: it is simply the number of times that one would find one was paying the EPS to buy the share. Thus a share priced at 250p with EPS 20p would show pe 12.5. In practice one can usually find on any day some shares with a pe as low as 3 or 4, whilst others may show as high as 50 or 60. Most companies will show in the range 8 to 20.

At first sight it may seem odd that you would be paying 50 times the EPS for one company, whilst you need pay only 4 times the EPS on another company. It is tempting to think that the lower the pe, the greater the bargain, but unfortunately that is not the case. My own 'rule-of-thumb' is to say 'Beware of a pe not in double digits (i.e. less than 10). It may not be a bargain but a company likely to go bust!'

The reasoning behind this is that EPS is an historic figure, based on the earnings of the last published annual accounts, the period for which may have ended over a year ago. The fact that a company made a profit in Year 1 does not mean it will automatically make a profit in Years 3, 4 or 5. Share prices on the stock exchange are determined by supply and demand, and will be low if investors' expectations are that a company is not likely to make good profits in the future. So EPS is history and share prices are based on future expectations. A good EPS last year with a low share price based on pessimism can easily result in the pe being a very small figure.

Working Capital Ratio (also known as **Current Ratio**)
Current assets/Current liabilities x 100 **(M/P)**

Working capital is the excess of current assets over current liabilities. Curiously, although it is a name known to all involved with accounts, it is rarely seen used on a balance sheet, as the Companies Act 1985 format insists on using the long-winded phrase 'Excess of current assets over current liabilities' (reversed where necessary).

Remembering that current assets are defined as being cash and assets held for conversion into cash, and current liabilities are those creditors falling due within one year of the balance sheet date, it will be realised that the greater the amount of working capital, the more comfortable will be the position of creditors. Nothing makes paying creditors more difficult than the absence of cash and anything one can turn into cash!

As a rule, we expect to see a working capital ratio of 150% or better, that is £3 in current assets for every £2 in current liabilities.

We cannot be dogmatic over such matters, though, as much depends on the nature of the business. Supermarkets, for example, seldom show any working capital in their balance sheets, for the simple reason that whilst their suppliers are happy to give them a month's credit, once the goods are in the store, they typically turn into cash within two weeks. A supermarket chief was once rash enough to boast that on opening a new store, most of the first month's takings could be taken to buy fixed assets, as the second month's takings would pay for the first month's purchases.

At the other end of the scale, a manufacturing business (say, one making bookcases) would need working capital of as much as 300%, as it would effectively have two stocks, one being the raw materials for manufacture (timber and glass) whilst the other was finished goods.

Quick Ratio (also known as Acid Test)

Debtors + cash/Current liabilities x 100 **(K + L/P)**

As a supplementary accounting ratio to the working capital ratio, and rather like putting a magnifying glass over this area, we calculate the quick ratio. We take all the current assets with the exception of stock. The idea seems to be that if we tried to pay all creditors quickly, we would have to choose between trying to sell more stock or collect existing debts. As people don't have to buy our goods but debtors do have to pay, the popular decision is to chase the debtors rather than try to turn more stock into cash.

It is a strong company that can cover its current liabilities with debtors and cash alone (i.e. one which can show 100% or more as its Quick Ratio), so we should not condemn a company just because its ratio is below that figure.

Liquidity Ratio

Cash/Current liabilities **(L/P)**

Even more stringent than quick ratio is the liquidity ratio. This measures the fraction of the current liabilities which the company is able to pay off with the cash shown in the balance sheet. Not surprisingly, we find 10% or less in most cases. By itself this ratio is not of much consequence, but as with all the above ratios, when we make comparisons over several years we often detect trends which may be welcome or unwelcome. But we must not read too much into a few figures: a large bank balance might be the result of selling investments last week in preparation for buying new equipment next week.

Turnover of Creditors and Credit Taken

Purchases/Trade creditors, alternatively Trade creditors x 12/Purchases **(B/N** or **N x 12/B)**

It is interesting to study the relationship of a company's purchases with its trade creditors. Dividing the former by the latter will disclose the number of times the creditors have been turned over during the year. Turn the same fraction upside down and multiply it by 12 and we see the number of months' credit taken on average. If you prefer the answer in units of weeks or days multiply by 52 or 365 respectively.

It is a sign of weakness if the period of credit taken by a company progressively increases over successive accounting periods, since it usually implies a lack of cash rather than mere laxity over issuing cheques. To make this figure as accurate as possible, we should be careful to take only those purchases which have been bought on credit terms, and only those creditors which relate to goods supplied as distinct from services rendered.

It is also important to bear in mind that, without further enquiry, we can never be sure that a balance sheet shows a typical month-end position. It would not be impossible, perhaps, for a company which normally took two months' credit, to pay off half its creditors on the eve of the balance sheet date, thus showing a position in which only one month's credit was being taken. Needless to say, the company would soon slip back to the two months' credit position. This sort of 'dressing up' the balance sheet might also be done by signing many cheques in favour of creditors and then not posting them for several weeks. These are the sort of things which auditors check before they sign a certificate declaring the accounts to show 'a true and fair view'.

Turnover of Debtors and Credit Given

Turnover/Debtors alternatively Debtors x 12/Turnover
(A/K or K x 12/A)

In a similar way to that adopted for creditors, one may ascertain the number of times debtors are turned over, or the period of credit given to them (or, perhaps more accurately, taken by the debtors).

Again we must ensure that the balance sheet entry for debtors does relate to sales and not to other matters. Both J. Sainsbury plc and Marks & Spencer plc show debtors in their balance sheets, but as it is well known that their retail trading is conducted for cash or credit cards (which effectively give them instant payment), there is no useful information to be gained from relating their debtors (which clearly must relate to other activities) to their retail sales. Similarly, with businesses which sell both for cash and on credit terms (e.g. builders' merchants), we must be careful to relate the debtors only to their credit sales.

A further complication arises with value added tax (VAT). VAT is a tax which registered traders have to collect for the Government whenever they make a sale. This tax is never regarded as part of their sales turnover, and throughout all accounting documents 'turnover' is taken to mean sales net of all taxes, whether those taxes are value added tax, entertainment tax or any other tax. However, the invoice charged to the customer has VAT added to it, and the debtor is therefore the greater. In comparing debtors which *include* VAT with sales which *exclude* VAT, a meaningful result will only be obtained if we exclude the VAT from the debtors before making the calculation. (The debtors figure is normally the only one on which we have to make an adjustment for VAT as other figures such as stock, purchases, expenses, creditors, will be shown in the accounts net of VAT)

The lengthening of the period of credit given is a sign of weakness, for it indicates that even allowing for changes in the volume of trade (or inflation), progressively more working capital has been tied up in debtors. As was indicated in the previous chapter, credit control should start before a sale is made, and credit should only be given to those worthy of it. When salesmen are paid by commission calculated on sales invoices, they are often a little too eager in selling on credit terms. One remedy is to base their commission on moneys collected from debtors, not simply the invoices issued.

Turnover of Stock

Cost of Sales/Stock alternatively Stock x 12/Cost of Sales **(C/J** or **J x 12/C)**

The relationship between stock and purchases is also an interesting one. Much depends on the nature of the trade, of course. Whereas a supermarket would expect to turn its stock over some twenty times or more in a year, a jeweller might turn his stock over only once in two years. Fishmongers, bakers, florists and fruiterers would hope to turn their stock over even faster than the supermarket whose tinned goods will be saleable long after their unsold stocks will have to be discarded.

We must be careful to compare like with like. Sales are recorded at selling price, stock at cost, so it is not sales but the cost of sales which is used to compare with the stock.

As with all other ratios, it is in the comparison with earlier periods that the value lies. 'If we only needed four weeks' stock on average last year, why have we now got six weeks' stock?' is the sort of question the manager will ask. There may well be a sensible answer, e.g. that the supplier has made a special offer at bargain prices so it was well worth 'stocking up', but since it is easier to buy goods than to sell them, we must be watchful that it is not the skill of the suppliers' salesmen which is the real cause of us tying up more money in stock than is really necessary. Surplus stock costs interest, takes up more space, and is possibly going to prove unfashionable or obsolete in many trades.

Capital Gearing
[Loan Capital/Loan capital + shareholders' funds] x 100 ([Q/Q+S] x 100)

An important concept in connection with the financing of companies is that of capital gearing (or leverage, as the Americans call it). Quite simply it is the relationship between the borrowed funds on which interest is payable and the proprietors' capital on which dividends will be paid, only if and when appropriate and possible.

In measuring the proprietors' capital we must include the profits which have been made but not distributed (usually referred to as 'retained profits') as well as the original share capital subscribed. There may also be other reserves to be included, such as any surplus on the revaluation of fixed assets. (Such unrealised profits always have to be placed in a 'revaluation reserve' which is not available for distribution as dividend, thence to be taken into profit and loss account only if and when actually realised on a sale.)

The loan capital may take any one of numerous names, but it is simply money borrowed at interest, long-term, for the financing of the business. It will always be shown at its full liability in the balance sheet. One expects to find that it will be repayable at a fixed date and at par value, though other variations are possible: it may get a premium on redemption, or it may be loan stock which is convertible to share capital at predetermined dates and at the option of the holder.

As with the measurement of the Return on Shareholders' Funds, we must be careful to see that we include a realistic value for the shareholders' funds. Fixed assets may be shown in the balance sheet at figures far below their market value, and such intangible items as goodwill, patents and trade marks may have been written off entirely, even if they were shown in the balance sheet earlier.

We use the expressions 'low geared' and 'high geared' to refer to companies where the loan capital is less than, and more than (respectively) the shareholders' funds. The effect of these alternative strategies is dealt with below.

If we are told that the gearing of a company is 25%, of the long term finance in the business, 25% is loan capital and the remaining 75% is shareholders' funds. Unfortunately, sometimes the calculation is made another way, taking loan capital as a percentage of shareholders' funds. In this case, the formula is *[Loan capital/Shareholders' funds] x 100*. That would mean that instead of the loan capital being £1,000 to every £3,000 of shareholders' funds, it would be £1,000 against every £4,000.

There are, unfortunately, no accounting standards when it comes to publishing accounting ratios, and since this ratio does get used both ways, it is important to understand the way in which it has been calculated before making comment – particularly in an examination.

The Practical Effect of Gearing

The effect of gearing is best explained in an example. Let us consider two companies, each using £200,000 in long term funds. One is high geared, borrowing most of this money, whilst the other is low geared, using shareholders' funds for the major part.

High geared company	£	**Low geared company**	£
Shareholders' funds	50,000	Shareholders' funds	150,000
Loan capital at 12%	150,000	Loan capital at 12%	50,000

In a normal year, the company's profits before interest charges may be £40,000. From this, the interest on the loan capital must be paid, and the balance is available for dividends to the shareholders:

Profit	40,000	Profit	40,000
Less loan interest at 12%	18,000	Less loan interest at 12%	6,000
Available for shareholders	22,000	Available for shareholders	34,000
Return on shareholders' funds:		Return on shareholders' funds:	
£22,000/£50,000 x 100 = 44%		£34,000/£150,000 x 100 = 23%	

In a good year, the profits might double to £80,000. The beauty of loan capital (as it then appears) is that we do not have to share our prosperity with those who lent us money. No bank manager was ever asked to increase his interest rates because the company had had a good year! The interest charges remain constant, therefore, and the full benefit of the extra profits passes to the shareholders:

Profit	80,000	Profit	80,000
Less loan interest at 12%	18,000	Less loan interest at 12%	6,000
Available for shareholders	62,000	Available for shareholders	4,000
Return on shareholders' funds:		Return on shareholders' funds:	
£62,000/£50,000 x 100 = 124%		£74,000/£150,000 x 100 = 49%	

After such a year, both directors and shareholders of the high geared company will be congratulating themselves on their earlier wisdom in the way they arranged the company finance, whilst those in the low geared company will be feeling they have in some way misjudged matters. How, given the same total funds and profits, can one company's shareholders achieve a near tripling of their return, whilst the other can do no more than a doubling?

Of course, normal years and good years are not the only possibilities, and the time may come when each company has a bad year, producing profits of no more than £10,000.

A return of only 3% to the shareholders of the low geared

Profits	10,000	Profits	10,000
Less loan interest at 12%	18,000	Less loan interest at 12%	6,000
Available for shareholders	(8,000)	Available for shareholders	4,000
Return on shareholders' funds: (£8,000)/£50,000 x 100 = -16%		Return on shareholders' funds: £4,000/£150,000 x 100 = 3%	

company may not seem much, but they will appreciate their directors' skills when they look at the fate of the high geared company. Loan interest is payable in both good and bad years, and lenders usually ensure that they have rights to appoint a receiver if their interest is not promptly met. Failure to pay the interest on the due date counts as a breach of covenant, entitling the receiver to move into the company to take both the outstanding interest and *the original loan capital as well!*

It will be seen, therefore, that whilst high geared companies will do well when fortune favours them, they can soon be in severe difficulties when they meet a bad year. Since the economy swings from boom to recession, history has many examples in recent decades when the companies who borrowed heavily were the first ones to collapse when recession struck.

Quite simply, the higher the gearing, the higher the risk. The company who never borrows money will never receive unwelcome letters from its bank manager, let alone face the prospect of having receivers at the door. And although the task of a receiver is only to collect the capital and interest for his principal by selling whatever is easiest to sell, few companies find that when the receivers leave, there is a viable business remaining.

There is no right or wrong amount of gearing for a business. Just as there are optimists and pessimists, so some businessmen are happy to work with a lot of borrowed money whilst others shudder at the thought. In practice, most small businesses rely heavily on having a bank overdraft and most large companies do not attempt to finance their activities with shareholders' funds alone. The question is always 'How much can be borrowed without risk?' The only answer must be 'None' for risk is part of all business activity. A low geared business borrows far less than its proprietor's capital, and accordingly even if half the assets are lost, the loss all falls on the proprietor. But a high geared company borrows far more than its proprietor's capital, and it does not need much loss before the assets are insufficient to meet the liabilities.

Bank managers constantly have to make risk assessments when asked for loans, and one of the first thoughts they will have is to compare the facilities sought with the person's capital. Risk assessment is a highly skilled business and it involves many matters beyond comparing the proposed loan and the person's capital, but the underlying truth must always be that 'the less the man has to lose, the more the creditor has to lose'.

10 Valuation methods

Although a balance sheet is probably one of the best-known documents in business, it must be clearly understood that it has many limitations: of no other document in the world of commerce can it be said that so many people expect so much – and are so disappointed to find they do not get it. Let us look briefly at what it is not. It is not a current market valuation of the business as a going concern; therefore it does not correctly state the current value of the shareholders' investment. It is not a collection of current market values of the individual assets; therefore it will not show the selling prices if the business is stopped and the assets are sold off piecemeal. It does not even include those liabilities which are likely to arise if the business is stopped, such as redundancy payments, since the theory is always that the balance sheet is constructed on a 'going concern' basis. It is not a valuation of the shareholders' funds on the basis either of the dividend paid in the last year, or the dividend expected to be paid in the next year; therefore it does not give any indication of what individual shareholders may expect to receive on the sale of their individual shareholdings. And finally, it does not indicate what the company might be worth to a prospective bidder and therefore gives no indication of what might happen to the share value on any takeover bid.

With all these negative aspects, why do we still use balance sheets? The answer must be that even with so many faults, we have nothing better to give an insight into the financial position of a company. (As has been mentioned earlier, the accountancy profession tried for several years to make 'current cost' balance sheets popular, but they were as popular as lead balloons.)

If we try to put a positive light on a balance sheet, we can expect to find within it all the liabilities of a business, both current and long-term (or deferred, as they are often called). But even then, we have to admit that for contingent liabilities (i.e. those which may arise) we will have to search through the voluminous notes which accompany the balance sheet, and for those liabilities which may arise if the going concern ceases to go, we can only use our imagination.

The current assets are usually helpfully recorded as conservative valuations – the stock at the lower of cost or net realisable value (i.e. expected selling price less costs of sale), the debtors at a figure which makes due provision for any bad or doubtful debts, and the cash counted to the last pound. It is the fixed assets which so often give difficulties. Starting with the basis of historic cost less accumulated depreciation (and one should read the accounting policies to see how the latter has been assessed), we then have to consider not only what items have been revalued, and when, but what have not. Company law requires that if fixed assets are overvalued, they must be reduced to reasonable figures; but if fixed assets are undervalued (perhaps because of inflation) there is no rule which makes the directors revalue them, though they are expected to express some comment about the fact that they are worth more than book values. Even property companies, whose assets can be free of the obligation to charge annual depreciation if they revalue periodically, seldom revalue more often than once in five years, so a revalued figure may be only a partial answer.

The plain fact is that a balance sheet is basically a record sheet which details the assets and liabilities, and the book values can hardly be used for any valuation purpose. Many examination questions ask candidates to work out the balance sheet value of a share (i.e. the value using the figures shown in the balance sheet for assets and liabilities) but this exercise does no more than to show that the candidate understands a little accountancy and has some basic mathematical ability.

Practical valuations take one of three forms, and sometimes a combination of two. They are the methods of break-up value, going concern and dividend yield.

Break-up value

If the balance sheet values mean little, how can we amend them to mean something? The easiest method is to amend them to current market values – in other words, to put them at what they would fetch if put up for sale. In the case of freehold and long leasehold property, this will usually be substantially greater than the balance sheet value. Plant and vehicles may fetch more or less than then balance sheet value: if the plant is specialised, its market value may be for scrap only. Current assets will usually show a fall in value, because although stock may normally sell above its cost, if we try to get rid of stock quickly, it means giving substantial discounts and selling below even the wholesale price. (The author once had to act as liquidator of a retail grocery stores. He cleared the entire stock in three days by offering '20% off everything'.)

One practical consideration is that when the money runs out in a business and there is insufficient to meet all claims (whether it be in respect of the liquidation of a company, or the bankruptcy of an individual), some creditors are given preferential treatment. You will learn the details of these later in your studies if necessary, but it will be sufficient here to note that they are mainly claims from staff (e.g. for salary) or from government departments (e.g. for taxes). They are referred to as being 'preferential creditors' and the basic rule is that until they have been paid in full, no other creditors get anything. Of course, there are always exceptions to rules and two exceptions have to be mentioned here: one is that any creditor who has a fixed (but not a floating) charge on an asset gets first claim on that asset, even before the preferential creditors; the other is that all costs of liquidation (e.g. legal costs and the liquidator's remuneration) also come to the top of the list.

Hopefully, therefore, when a company goes into liquidation there will be enough to meet all creditors and then return to the shareholders some if not all of their original investment. Any shortfall must fall first on the shareholders and then on the ordinary (unsecured) creditors. Sadly, in practice, one sees many cases where the funds are insufficient to pay even the preferential claims in full.

The following example shows how a break-up value is calculated.

Grotty Engineering Co Ltd
Balance sheet – 31 December ....

	£	£
Fixed assets		
Freehold property, at cost		50,000
Machinery, at cost	100,000	
Less Depreciation	5,000	55,000
		105,000
Current assets		
Stock	20,000	
Debtors	12,000	
Cash	100	
	32,100	
Creditors: amounts falling due withion one year		
Trade creditors	37,000	
Bank overdraft	3,100	
	40,100	
Net current liabilities		(8,000)
		97,000
Creditors:amounts falling due after more than one year		
Debentures (unsecured)		50,000
		47,000
Share capital and reserves		
Called up share capital	10,000	
Retained profits	37,000	47,000

The freehold property has a market value of £120,000. The machinery is valued for sale at £18,500. Stock is expected to fetch £14,000, debtors are estimated to produce only £9,500 and the costs of liquidation may be assumed to be £3,000. If £4,500 of the total creditors shown are preferential, calculate how much each share may receive after the company is liquidated.

The result of liquidating the company and selling the assets piecemeal is shown below:

	£	£
Freehold property		120,000
Machinery		18,500
Stock		14,000
Debtors		9,500
Cash		100
		162,100
Less Costs of liquidation		3,000
		159,100
Less Preferential creditors		4,500
		154,600
Less Debentures	50,000	
Creditors (balance)	32,500	
Bank overdraft	3,100	85,600
Available for shareholders		69,000

With 10,000 shares in issue, each would therefore receive £69,000/10,000 = £6.90.

By contrast, the somewhat meaningless balance sheet figure was £47,000/10,000 = £4.70.

It is important to note the priority in sequence which the various liabilities have – liquidation costs first, then preferential creditors, followed by unsecured creditors. Shareholders always come last.

If the debentures had been secured by a fixed charge (e.g. a mortgage on the property), they would have had a first claim on that asset: had the sales proceeds been insufficient to cover the liability in full, the excess claim would have been an unsecured liability. However, if the debentures had been secured by a floating charge, they would have had first claim on the sum of £154,600; that is, the preferential creditors would have been ahead of them. The sequence of claims has no effect when there are sufficient funds to meet all creditors' claims, but it is of vital importance when funds are insufficient – which is invariably the case in examination questions!

Going concern value

A going concern is nearly always worth more than the sum of its tangible assets less its liabilities. This is not really surprising, because every business has had to be organised and created and there will always been an advantage in having a business ready-made and operating, as compared with having to procure premises, buy fixed assets, order stock, and so on. Not the least advantage of a going business is that one can expect to have customers on the first day of ownership. No one who has not tried starting a business from nothing can even imagine the awful feeling of having everything one needs for a successful business – except the customers! In such cases, only two factors will solve the problem – time and good luck.

If a going concern is worth more than its constituent parts, how do we show this in the balance sheet? The answer is that we do not try to. The balance sheet is not a current market value of the business. The only time that it will become one is if a business is bought as a going concern. The individual assets will then be entered in the balance sheet at their agreed buying price and the balance of the total purchase price will be described as 'goodwill'. A judge once described goodwill as the probability that old customers will return to the old place of business. The existence of goodwill means not only that the business is a going concern but also that it must be operating efficiently and making a profit, for no business can survive for long whilst making a loss (unless it is subsidised by the government).

Suppose that the Grotty Engineering Co Ltd is making a net profit of £8,000 per year. If an investor regards 10% as being a reasonable return on capital in such a business, he will consider the company to be worth £8,000 x 100/10, or £80,000. If he could buy all the shares (and obviously he would need to own at least 51% of the shares to obtain control) he would be willing to pay

£80,000/10,000, or £8.00 each. This is in excess of the £6.90 break- up value shown above, because of the existence of goodwill. Valuing the whole company at £80,000 when the net tangible assets were only £69,000 would mean that goodwill was valued at the difference of £11,000.

If all the shares were purchased for £80,000, the goodwill would not appear in the balance sheet for it is accounting convention today that balance sheets should not normally show such an asset. The only time one would see such an entry would be if the business were bought by the person himself, rather than the person buying the shares of the company which owned the business: the opening balance for that individual might then show an entry for £11,000 goodwill at cost. Since goodwill is such an intangible asset, accounting standards today require that the only time goodwill may appear in a balance sheet is when it has been acquired by purchase: it should then be written off as quickly as possible, and there must be no attempt to revalue it upwards or to introduce 'home-made' goodwill.

Finally, suppose the Grotty Engineering Co Ltd only earns £5,000 per year. On the basis of an investor requiring a 10% yield, this indicates a going concern value of only £50,000 for the business – yet the net assets show a break-up value of £69,000.

This is the situation in which 'asset strippers' appear. It is often possible to find a company whose net assets per share are worth considerably more than the market price of the share. If someone could buy the shares at £5.00 each (reflecting a going concern value of £50,000), it should not be difficult to sell the assets piecemeal, pay off the liabilities, and have a comfortable profit at the end of the operation. Of course, the mere fact that people know this can be done often means that the market price of a share tends to stay within a reasonable distance of its net asset value. If a company makes neither profit nor loss, the shareholders do not regard the shares as being worthless.

Dividend yield value

In practice, a company seldom pays out to its shareholders in dividend the entire profits of each year. Whilst the profits earned may be a suitable basis for valuing the shares when a person is going to buy the entire share capital (enabling them to take control and therefore the entire profits each year), if an investor owns something less than 51% of the share capital, what determines the value of that person's investment (in the absence of any take-over bid) is simply the dividends which that shareholder will receive.

If the Grotty Engineering Co Ltd pays out £4,000 by way of dividends, it does not make much difference whether this is paid from profits of £8,000 or £5,000, for £4,000 is all the shareholders will receive.

If a shareholder feels that 8% is the appropriate yield on such an investment, the capital value of his shareholding will be 100/8 times his dividend. Thus, if the shareholder has 100 shares, the dividend will be 100/10,000 x £4,000 = £40, and the capital value will be £40 x 100/8 = £5.00 each.

With minority shareholdings, where the individual shareholder has no power to control the company nor even to liquidate it, the dividend yield value is the only relevant one to consider.

Conclusion

In practice, all the above methods (with the exception of the balance sheet value) are used. The fact that stock exchange prices of shares fluctuate daily, even in the absence of any news from the company about its activities, indicates that the valuation of shares is a matter which involves many facts other than purely the asset values or the profit-making ability of the company. The supply of and demand for the shares on any day is the dominating factor in determining the market price.

In all the above examples, taxation has been ignored in all forms, but in real life it cannot be ignored. On break-up value, for example, there is little attraction in making a capital profit if it is all going to be taken by the taxman! Capital gains tax is very complicated, involving base values and indexation, and frequently there will be a 'double-decker' slice of tax: the company may have to pay tax on the gains it makes selling the assets, and the investor may then be liable to capital gains tax on the overall gain he makes on his investment purchase and liquidation.

Hard bargaining by the interested parties, coupled to their optimism or pessimism as to how matters will turn out, will be the determining factor in practice, but the underlying principles which have been described here are to be found in all such situations – and in many accountancy examinations.

11 Specialised presentations

As has been explained earlier, the Companies Act 1985 lays down the format which must be adopted for balance sheets and profit and loss accounts which are to be presented to shareholders and filed with the Registrar of Companies each year. There is, however, an overriding requirement that such accounts show 'a true and fair view': if such is not possible by the use of such formats, the accountant is at liberty to use whatever format he feels most appropriate. Thus for companies which do not trade (e.g. trade associations and charities) the expressions 'turnover' and 'cost of sales' are hardly appropriate, and what will be far more interesting to the members of such companies will be a list of the sources whence their funds came and the expenses or donations to which they have been put.

The Companies Act does not, of course, apply to sole traders and partnerships, though it is inevitable that many of the terms used in company accounts find their way also into those of unincorporated businesses, e.g. fixed assets, current assets, gross profit. It is not possible in a general introduction to accounting (and this book is no more than that) to detail all the possible forms in which accounts may be presented, but the following are the more basic forms you may expect to meet.

Manufacturing Accounts

In cases where the business is manufacturing a product, its cost of goods sold is not merely one or two items (as one would see in a retailer's profit and loss account) but a large number of different expenses amounting, in total, to the cost of running a factory and changing the form of the materials which pass through it. To try and bring all such expenses into a trading account would be cumbersome (if the details of the different expenses were to be shown) or give little information (if the details were all lost in a single figure of total expenditure). Just as we separate the cost of sales of a trader from his other expenses, so we can go back one further stage and use another account – which we will call the 'manufacturing account' – to calculate the cost of the goods produced by the factory. This cost of manufacture is then our single figure of purchases, in effect, being the total cost of goods taken into our selling operation.

In practice, one may often see the business buying purchases from other suppliers to sell, as well as taking the output of its own factory. Consider an ice cream company. It may be easier to buy in the wafer biscuits to sell with its own manufactured ice cream than to try and start its own bakery. In such cases, the cost of sales in the profit and loss account will show purchases from that supplier as well as its own cost of manufacturing.

An example of a manufacturing account appears in Figure 24.

The cost which is being taken into the profit and loss account is the cost of the finished goods which have been manufactured in the year: many factories will have part-finished goods at the end of the year which obviously cannot be sold in that state, so the value attributed to them (work in progress) is left in the manufacturing account and carried forward to the following year. The figure of £7,996,400 therefore represents the cost of the finished goods only which have been produced by the factory in the year.

Some people express surprise that in a manufacturing account we do not normally have a figure of profit or loss disclosed on the manufacturing operation. Normally, we merely transfer the cost of the operation, as shown in the example. If we can establish a value (as distinct from a cost) for the output of the factory, we can calculate a figure of profit or loss on the manufacturing activities. For example, if the cost of £7,888,773 related to an output of 42,000 whatnots which are valued at £200 each, we could take the figure of £8,400,000 as being the value of the factory's output for the year and declare a profit on manufacturing of (£8,400,000 – £7,996,400) £403,600. This would then be taken to the profit and loss account as

Tinned Foods Ltd
Manufacturing Account
Year ended 30 September ....

	£	£
Stock of raw materials, 1 Oct	583,909	
Add Purchases in year	3,359,171	
	3,943,080	
Less Stock of raw materials, 30 Sept	675,320	3,267,760
Factory wages		2,979,675
Factory rent and rates		761,153
Repairs to factory		73,118
Depreciation of machinery		843,008
Heating, lighting and power		104,872
General factory expenses		93,714
		8,123,300
Add Work in progress, 1 Oct		564,900
		8,688,200
Less Work in progress, 30 Sept		691,800
Cost of manufacturedr goods in year, transferred to profit and loss account		7,996,400

Figure 24. A manufacturing account

a separate profit, and we would use the £8,400,000 figure as being the effective cost of purchases from the factory.

By doing so, of course, we would not show a greater total profit for the company as a whole, but would merely be splitting the total profit between a figure of profit on manufacturing and a profit on selling – a somewhat arbitrary operation some might say.

Note that the factory will be likely to have a figure of opening and closing work in progress (part-finished goods) as well as its own opening and closing stocks of raw materials: these will be quite distinct from the opening and closing stocks of finished goods, though all three figures will appear in current assets in the balance sheet each year.

Income and Expenditure Accounts

The easiest way to describe income and expenditure accounts is to suggest that they are profit and loss accounts for organisations which do not seek to make profits, e.g. professional organisations, but nevertheless have to explain what has taken place in the year.

If the income has exceeded expenditure, the balance is not termed a profit but referred to as being the excess of income over expenditure, or, more shortly, the surplus for the year. Conversely, an excess of expenditure over income may be termed a deficit for the year.

Sometimes a small non-trading organisation may present its members with a receipts and payments account, which is no more than a summary of the cash transactions of the year, such as will be seen in the cash book (see Figure 29).

Such a statement suffers from the defect that unless a transaction has been completed by the receipt or payment of cash, it will not appear in the account. Thus if the professional organisation has held an annual dinner and a member still owes £60 for tickets, that sum will not be brought into account since it is neither a receipt nor a payment.

To present a receipts and payments account as the summary of the year's activities therefore offends against the fundamental accounting concept of accruals.

An income and expenditure account brings into account accruals (both of expenses and income) and the £60 owing for the annual dinner tickets above would be included in the ticket sales accordingly.

One of the skills which have to be cultivated is good presentation in accounting, for communication will always be improved if the presentation is skilful. Thus we do not merely put income at the top of the page and expenditure at the foot: we try to bring together those items which are clearly related. This is seen in Figure 25, where the income and expenses of the annual dinner are brought together, as are the garden party and Christmas draw income and expenses.

Although the income and expenditure account closely resembles a profit and loss account, nowhere will we expect to find the words

The Village Green Cricket Club
Income and Expenditure Account
Year ended 31 January ....

		£	£
Income			
Subscriptions			12,300
Investment income			834
Garden party income		852	
Garden party expenses		503	349
Christmas raffle income		741	
Christmas raffle expenses		97	644
Donation from A. Non			1,000
			15,217
Expenditure			
Staff salaries		6,462	
Travelling expenses		5,848	
Office expenses		2,583	
Depreciation of equipment		852	
Accountancy fees		350	
Bank charges		218	
Annual dinner cost	780		
Annual dinner ticket sales	625	155	
General expenses		92	16,560
Deficit for the year			1,343

Figure 25. An income and expenditure account

'profit' or 'loss'. The expenditure will include any expenses relating to the period, regardless of whether or not they have been paid. Similarly, subscriptions will also be brought in if they are expected to be received later. (Since the subscriptions of most societies are payable in advance, and at the beginning of the society's accounting year, it normally follows that, apart from any new members, any subscriptions outstanding at the balance sheet date will then be a year overdue. This period alone casts doubt on whether they will ever be received, so in many societies debtors are not brought in for overdue subscriptions, and the members concerned are informed that their membership has lapsed. Indeed, most professional bodies exclude people from membership if their subscription has not been paid within a few months of it becoming due – and charge a hefty fee if the member wishes to rejoin!

Organisations which do not trade for profit do not normally have the large amounts of capital needed for trading enterprises, since they seldom have much equipment, stock or debtors to finance. Their capital has usually been the result of voluntary donations when they started, coupled with surplus income over the years. The usual title given to this capital is 'accumulated fund', though other names are met in practice. If a deficit arises, this is carried to the accumulated fund and therefore reduces it, just as a surplus would increase it.

Charities have recently been required by the Charity Commission (a government department) to identify what part, if any, of their funds have a restricted use (i.e. are available for specific purposes only) and to distinguish between restricted and unrestricted funds and label them accordingly. A new term of 'designated funds' has also arisen for use when the charity's trustees have 'earmarked' funds for a particular purpose, but are still able to discard such voluntary restriction on their application.

Partnership Accounts

Partnerships are not recognised as separate legal bodies but are merely two or more persons who have agreed to carry on business in common with a view of profit. They may share such profit (or loss) in any way they agree, and in the absence of specific agreement will be required to share equally.

In recent years the age-old restrictions on numbers allowed to be partners in any firm (20 normally, but only 10 for banking partnerships) has been discarded by law in most cases, and there is now no limit on the numbers who may be partners if their business is a recognised profession. However, the difficulties and dangers of being one of, say, 400 partners in a firm has become apparent, for

Hickory, Dickory and Dock
Appropriation Account
Year ended 31 March ....

		£	£
Net profit for the year, from P&L Account			215,976
Partners' salaries:			
Hickory		65,000	
Dickory		50,000	
Dock		35,000	150,000
			65,976
Interest on capital:			
Hickory	8% on £60,000	4,800	
Dickory	8% on £45,000	3,600	
Dock	8% on £20,000	1,600	10,000
			55,976
Share of profit:			
Hickory	40%	22,390	
Dickory	35%	19,592	
Dock	25%	13,994	55,976

Figure 26. A partnership appropriation account

every partner is bound by the acts and omissions of his fellow partners. One bad judgment by a single partner could make all 400 bankrupt!

The only differences between a sole trader's account and that of a partnership is that the profit of the latter is shared between the partners in some agreed manner: sometimes this is a simple ratio, in other cases it can involve partners having individual salaries, interest on their capital (and even drawings) and a final splitting by ratio. The total profit taken by each partner is then carried to his current account, against which his drawings are charged. Note that drawings are never charged to profit and loss account, even if part of them are described as being partners' salaries.

An example of a more complicated sharing of partnership is shown in Figure 26.

The rate of interest, shown as 8% above, would have to be agreed by all partners, as would be the percentage rates in which the final figure of profit would be shared.

In the balance sheet, the minimum requirement would be for each partner to be given his own capital account. Frequently the partners will agree to maintain a minimum figure of capital within the firm, and this figure would then be kept as a constant figure on which the interest would be calculated. All other items, as shown above, and the partners' drawings, would be shown on current accounts. These may then be summarised on a separate sheet and just two figures taken to the balance sheet, one being the total of the partners' capital accounts and the other the total of the partners' current accounts. Such a summary is shown in Figure 27.

There is, of course, no objection to including all this detail on the partnership balance sheet, but it will be realised that the more numerous the partners, the greater will be the inclination to show only the totals there.

	Hickory	**Dickory**	**Dock**	**Total**
	£	£	£	£
Capital Accounts	60,000	45,000	20,000	125,000
Current Accounts				
Balance b/fwd	11,538	19,402	7,811	
Partners' salaries	65,000	50,000	35,000	
Share of profit	22,390	19,592	13,994	
		98,928	88,994	56,805
Less Drawings	89,538	76,935	47,706	
Balance c/fwd	9,390	12,059	9,099	30,548

Figure 27. Partnership capital and current accounts

Conclusion

In the world of business, there are as many diverse types of account as there are types of business. In the space of a general introduction to the subject, it has not been possible to do more than give simple illustrations of those most often met.

Specialised businesses need specialised accounts, however, and the annual accounts of, say, an insurance company or a building society have little in common with those of a manufacturing or trading company.

Fortunately there is normally no difficulty in obtaining current examples of balance sheets and profit and loss accounts, for quite apart from the legal obligation of companies to file annual accounts with the Registrar of Companies (where copies on microfiche may be inspected and taken away, or obtained by post, for a small fee), it is customary for public companies to use their annual accounts as advertising material. Not only are they often published in daily newspapers but public companies are always willing, without charge, to send a copy of their last Annual Report by post to anyone requesting this.

Public companies do not disclose all their accounting information to the public, and the details published are frequently the minimum required by the Companies Act 1985. The accounting profession's own disclosure rules are often more demanding than the law, and the notes that accompany the balance sheet and profit and loss account often run to 20 or more pages. Although disclosure of the directors' names and individual shareholdings has to be given, and details of the directors' remuneration in bands, it is often a guessing game as to which director got what remuneration. The highest remuneration to any one director must be shown, but no name has to be attached to the figure.

Public libraries and colleges usually maintain a big collection of Annual Reports.

Although accounting procedures start with basic records, the quill pen of former years giving way, progressively, to mechanised systems and now to computerised accounting systems, the end product is by no means a boring set of updated figures each year. Quite apart from the changes brought about by new legislation and practices, most public companies endeavour to show their shareholders and other readers colour pictures of their management, their staff and their products each year. So voluminous and costly have these become in many cases that the practice has emerged in recent years of replacing the full Annual Report by a simplified and much shortened Annual Review: this is quite legal provided that the individual shareholder is offered a full report on request.

12 Double-entry book keeping methods

Today it is uncommon to find any business keeping its financial records as 'a full set of books'. The small business need keep only minimal records (e.g. an analysed cash book, detailing all bank transactions) and can rely on the professional accountant to prepare the year-end profit and loss account and balance sheet. Large and medium sized businesses are invariably found to be using computers, and ever since it was possible to buy a personal computer for as little as £2,000, there has been a move towards the computer by even small firms. Today, it is possible to buy a complete computer and printer for considerably less, so small wonder that even domestic financial records get computerised.

The principles of double-entry book-keeping have apparently been with us for something like 500 years, so it is a well-tried and well-tested system. The theory that every transaction has two aspects, which we term the 'debit' and the 'credit' aspects, goes through all financial records. The beauty of the computerised system is that a single keyboard entry will deal with both aspects simultaneously, and, furthermore, remove from the operator the chore of having to add up all the figures – never a popular job! The computer system, in fact, may be regarded as keeping quadruple-entry records, for in addition to the normal debits and credits it will give us the appropriate control (or total) accounts for debtors and creditors, and produce the data for the VAT returns which most businesses must make.

An understanding of what double-entry book-keeping is all about is still necessary, though, if we are to understand the reasoning behind any accounting system. The computer operator's fingers may flash across the keyboard, but if he or she is unversed in the basic theories, they will come to an abrupt halt when, as is sometimes needed, a journal entry must be made in terms of a debit and a credit.

What follows in this chapter must rate as one of the quickest guides ever written on the subject of books of account.

Figure 28 shows the basic ledger account, which is the building block on which all book-keeping systems depend. There are two identical sides: the left-hand side is always called the 'debit' side, the right hand one the 'credit' side. In the case of a customer who is buying goods on credit from a shop, we would show the sales made to him on the debit side and the cash subsequently received from him on the credit side. If the sum of the debit entries exceeds the sum of the credit entries, the excess is termed a debit balance and we refer to that customer as being a debtor. We have similar ledger accounts for the people from whom the business buys goods, but in those the goods received would be shown on the credit side and the cash subsequently paid to the supplier would be shown on the debit

A. CUSTOMER							
DATE	DETAILS		AMOUNT	DATE	DETAILS		AMOUNT
3 Jan	Sales		25.00	31 Jan	Cash		25.00
	Debit Side				Credit Side		

Figure 28. A ledger account

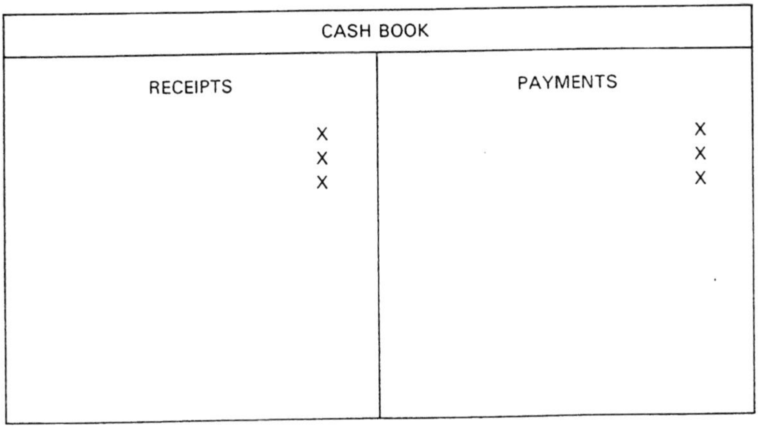

Figure 29. The cash book

side. Suppliers who had delivered goods but not received payment for them would have credit balances and be known as creditors.

A particular ledger account which is much used is shown in Figure 29. It is the cash book. It is usually the most used ledger account in the whole system and in a manual system it will nearly always be kept as a separate book. Often there are several cash books in a business. The main one will be recording the receipts and payments of cash we keep on our bank account. Logically, it would be more appropriate to call it a bank book, but this title is never used. Other cash books will be used for the small funds of cash which are kept by various members of staff to meet lesser expenses: being small cash accounts, they are called the 'petty cash books'. In all cases, receipts are recorded on the left or debit side, and payments on the right or credit side.

The petty cash book (often several) usually has extra columns on the right hand side, as seen in Figure 30. This is to enable the various expenses to be analysed under one of several headings after they have been entered in the total payments column. Thus column 1 might be for postage, column 2 for stationery, column 3 for travelling expenses, and so on. The petty cash book will be 'fed' by

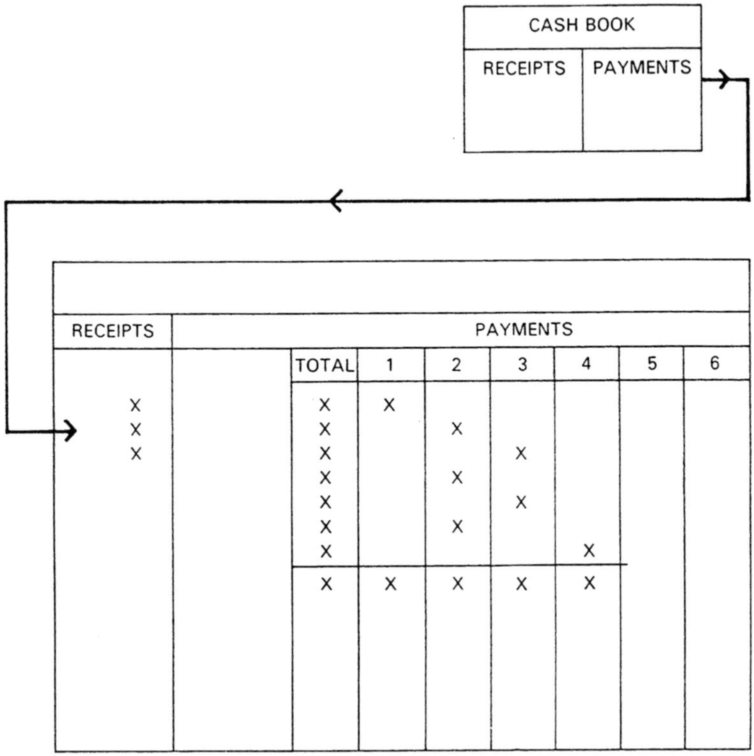

Figure 30. The petty cash book

money being withdrawn from the bank (and shown as a payment in the cash book) and placed in the petty cash funds (usually kept in a cash box) and recorded as a receipt in the petty cash book. The arrows show the posting entry.

Having shown how cash transactions are recorded, we must now look at the sales on credit. If our customers are allowed to buy goods on credit, it is important that we keep records to show who owes how much. We do this by summarising all our sales on credit (which will be shown on individual invoices) in a special book, known as the sales day book. This is not a ledger but merely a convenient summary. In some systems it is known as the sales journal. This is shown in Figure 31, together with the set of ledger accounts which relate to the customers. These we keep in a separate book or binder (if loose leaf) and term the sales ledger. Again, the arrows show the postings.

In a similar way, but with the entries kept on the opposite sides in the ledger accounts, we have a book in which we record our purchases on credit, and the moneys we owe to our suppliers. The ledger accounts for the latter we term the purchases or bought ledger. They are shown in Figure 32. There is sometimes a single column book, similar to the sales day book, in which we record our purchases of goods for resale: in such cases we call it the purchases day book or purchases journal. It is more common, however, to find that we are recording not only the purchases of goods for resale but also the incurring of other expenses on credit, e.g. purchases of stationery, orders for advertising, for carriage, and for lighting, heating and power charges. Therefore we normally use an analysed book, in the form shown in Figure 32, so that we can record everything in the total column, and then analyse the charges under appropriate headings, e.g. goods for resale (known simply as purchases), and suitable expense headings such as stationery, advertising, carriage, lighting, heating and power, and so on. We call this the bought day book. The appearance is very similar to the petty cash book (Figure 30) except that there is no left hand (debit) column. Everything bought on credit is therefore listed in the bought day book, and analysed under the column appropriate to it. Each individual invoice is posted to the relevant supplier's account in the bought ledger.

There is one more ledger. This is the private ledger, also known as the nominal or impersonal ledger. Whereas the sales and bought ledgers deal with people (the customers who buy goods on credit and owe the business money, and the suppliers supply goods and services and are owed money), the private ledger deals only with intangible things – the various types of income and expenses, and long-term assets and liabilities of the business. This is portrayed in Figure 33.

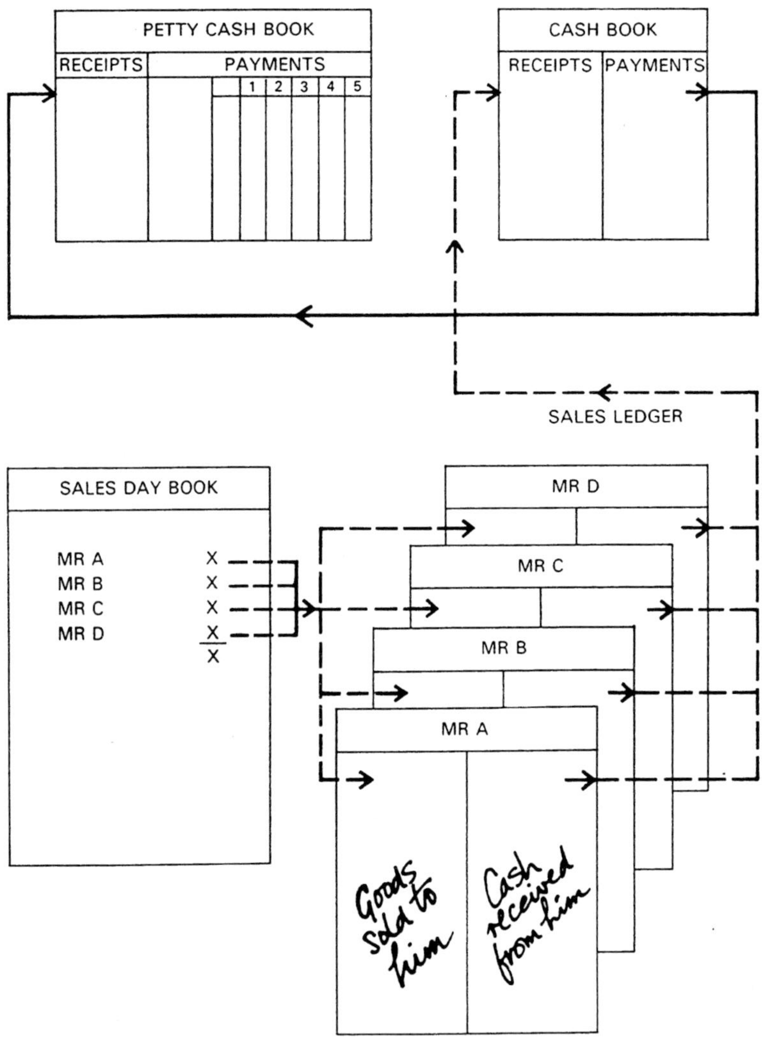

Figure 31. The sales ledger

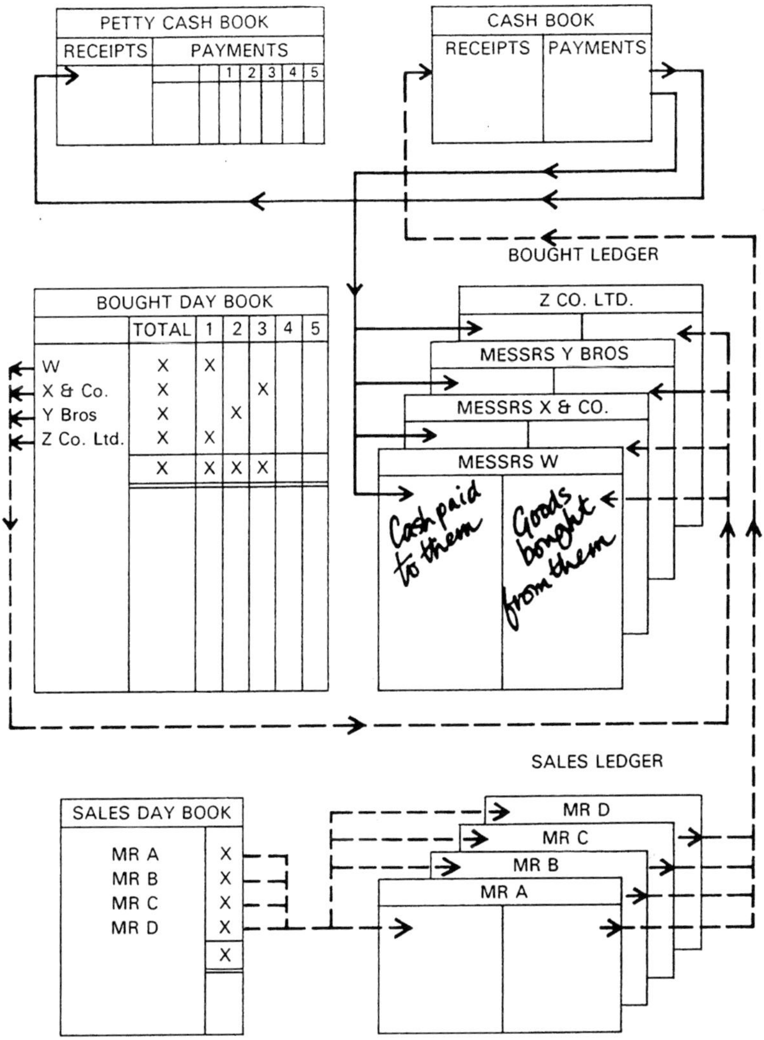

Figure 32. The bought ledger

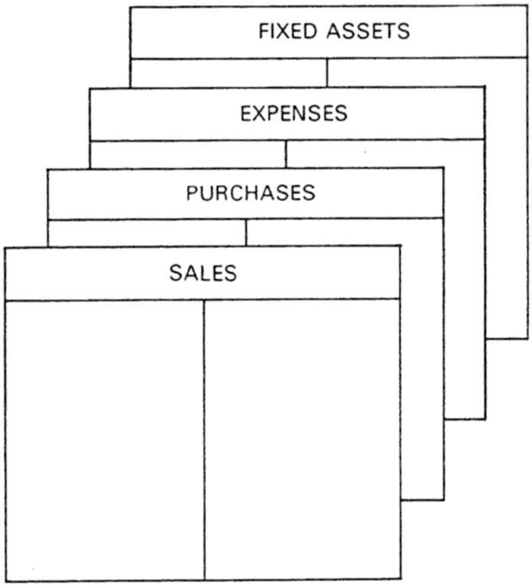

Figure 33. The private ledger
(also known as the nominal or impersonal ledger)

The private ledger gets its name from the fact that if anything should be kept private, it is obviously the contents of this ledger! Here is the summary of all the activities of the business – its sales, purchases, expenses and assets. Whereas a competitor could ascertain (albeit with some difficulty) the sales of a business from copies of all sales invoices, or from all the ledger sheets in the sales ledger, in the private ledger every single account is a convenient summary of some facet of the business.

Private ledgers are for obvious reasons normally kept in the office safe!

The use of the private ledger is illustrated in Figure 34. It pulls together all the 'loose ends' of the recording systems. Double-entry book-keeping is so called because for every transaction there are two aspects recorded. These are the debit and the credit aspects, but may be regarded as being the 'plus' and 'minus' aspects. Thus when

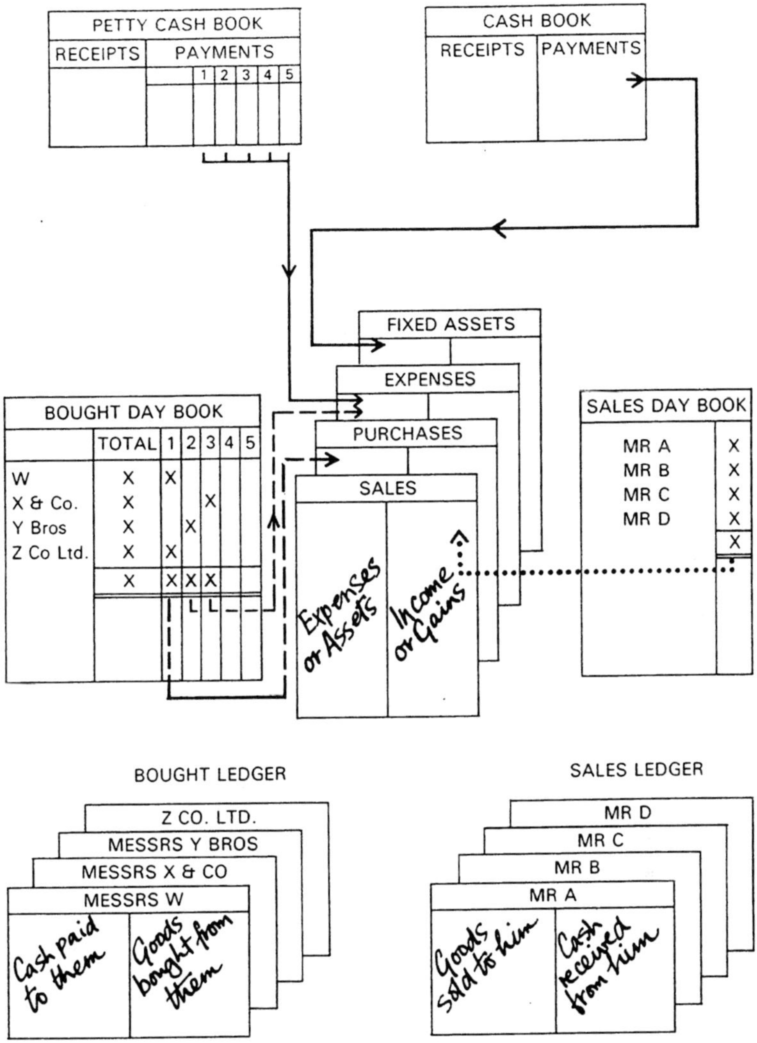

Figure 34. Completing the double entry

TYPE	EXAMPLE		POSTING RULE
REAL	CASH STOCK	DR	RECEIPTS
		CR	PAYMENTS
PERSONAL	MR A XYZ LTD	DR	RECEIVER
		CR	GIVER
NOMINAL	SALES RENT	DR	EXPENSE
		CR	GAIN

Figure 35. The rules of double entry
(Every debit must have a credit)

cash is expended on postage, our postage account should show the 'plus' for the expense, and the cash book (or petty cash book) should show the 'minus' for the cash balance going down.

The theoretical rules of double-entry are summarised in Figure 35.

All ledger accounts can be divided into three groups: real accounts, which deal with real or tangible items, such as cash or machinery; personal accounts, which deal with persons, such as our customers and suppliers; and nominal accounts which are all the others, recording expenses and gains. If you have difficulty in working out whether some ledger posting is a debit or a credit, it usually helps to think back to the cash aspect, and remember that 'every debit must have a credit' (and vice versa). Thus if money is received for a sale made for cash, it will be recorded in the cash book as a receipt on the left or debit side. Therefore the other half of the entry must be a credit entry in the sales account. Similarly, if a payment is made for postage, it will be a credit entry in the (petty) cash book and a debit entry in the postage account. Both the sales account and the postage account will be ledger accounts in the private ledger.

The Trial Balance

Bearing in mind that every debit must have a credit, it will be realised that a useful check on the accuracy of book-keeping will be to see if the total debits entered in the books of account amount to the same as the total credits. In fact we do this more simply by taking the net balance on the ledger accounts. If Mr A has been debited with £50 for goods sold to him on credit, and has been credited with £50 cash he has paid for them, there will be no balance on his account and we can ignore it as being a completed transaction.

The list of net balances which we take out is known as a trial balance. A simple one relating to an accountant's practice might appear as follows:

	£	£
Cash	512	
Fixed assets	5,128	
Fees received		58,156
Salaries	22,147	
Office expenses	11,956	
Mr A (a debtor)	752	
B Ltd (a creditor)		152
Capital account		14,137
Drawings	31,950	
	72,445	72,445

The profit and loss account and balance sheet which can be drawn up from this trial balance appears in Figure 36 but you may like to test your accounting ability by writing up these items before turning the page.

Errors not disclosed in a trial balance

A trial balance is a useful check on the accuracy of the entries in a set of books. If one finds that it does not balance, it is clear that somewhere there are one or more debits not matched by corresponding credits, or vice versa. You may even discover one debit with two matching credits! The most usual cause of a trial balance not balancing is that some cash book entry has not had 'the other half' of the entry made, e.g. a cash payment has been made which has not been posted as a debit to an expense account. Having ascertained the precise difference between the debits and credits, a careful search through the books will often reveal the item causing the trouble, as the trial balance will be out of balance by that amount.

Useful though a trial balance is to give reassurance, it cannot reveal an error which has arisen through a transaction not being recorded anywhere. There is clearly no system which can say 'I'm short of both a credit and a debit'.

A trial balance will also not reveal mispostings. If Mr C has paid us £100 and we post it to the credit of Mr D's account, the trial balance will balance but the accounts of both Mr C and Mr D will show wrong balances.

Finally, a trial balance will not reveal compensating errors. An error of £10 in an addition (known as a cast) in, say, the sales day book can by co-incidence be offset by an error of £10 in the cast of some ledger account (e.g. travelling expenses).

When a trial balance does not balance (i.e. where the total debit balances are not the same as the total credit balances), the first step should be to check the arithmetic (i.e. recast the columns): the second should be to look for a missing entry, which may reveal itself as being a transaction of which only one half has been posted. A dividend received, for example, may have been recorded in the cash book properly (receipts side) but not posted anywhere in the private ledger, perhaps because the book-keeper did not know where to post it. In Figure 28, you will see that on each side of the ledger account there is a narrow column between the columns for details and amount. This is known as the folio column and is used to cross reference the postings. Each ledger account (including the cash book) has such columns, as do the day books, and in it one enters at the time of posting the number of the ledger page to which the other half of the entry has been made, or, conversely, whence it has come. Thus the page of the cash book might be 'CB 36' and this would be inserted on the ledger account for dividends received. Similarly, if that account was 'D 8', that reference would be shown in the folio column of the cash book. A quick way of looking for unposted items, therefore, is to run one's eye down the folio columns, looking for a blank which will indicated an unposted entry.

One practical tip which is often time saving is to remember that when a figure is transposed (i.e. when a multi-digit number is copied with the digits in a difference sequence, such as 312 copied as 321, the difference will always be 9, or the digits of the difference will always add up to 9. Thus if 7,151 is copied as 1,715, the difference will be 5,436. Add together the digits 5 + 4 + 3 + 6 and we get 18. Add the digits 1 + 8 and we get 9. Whenever you find a difference on a trial balance where the digits of the difference add up to 9, consider the possibility that an error of transposition has been the cause.

If all else fails, the only way to locate the difference may be to check every posting and cast in the whole system. This is a laborious task, and if the difference is very small (e.g. £1) it may well be felt that it is not worth the effort. In that case, the difference is added to or subtracted from an account such as general expenses.

Conclusion

Few people other than accountants and book-keepers need to have great skills in book-keeping, and for the reasons already stated, few large companies maintain two-sided ledger accounts. The 'counting house' of the last century has become the computer centre. Handwritten records today usually exist only in the smaller businesses, or at the 'top of the tree' where the professional accountant writes up the private ledger as the last link in the chain. Intermediate links in the chain are sometimes barely recognisable as being ledger accounts – our computerised bank statements bear witness to this.

The personal computer is not only much faster than a hand written record, it is more accurate in most cases. The computer will not produce a trial balance which does not balance, and its power to perform arithmetic is unsurpassed. Although its records are created in invisible magnetic form, they appear instantly readable on the monitor screen and the printed reports at the end of each period make up a full record in hard copy form for reference. The only danger lies in relying too much on the hardware, for if damaged (sometimes unwittingly by problems on mains power) let alone stolen, a business can lose all its records in a moment. It is always vital, therefore, that back-up copies of data be regularly taken on disks or tape: merely taking such extra copies of the recorded data is not by itself enough, for if left with the computer (as I have seen done), a fire overnight will destroy everything. Always ensure that such back-ups are taken away from the business premises for safety.

Whilst the art of double-entry book-keeping is no longer regarded as a necessary skill of any aspiring businessman or manager, it is still important when using final accounts (i.e. balance sheets and profit and loss accounts) to remember that the basic principles of double-entry have not been lost. A profit must therefore result in an increased asset or a diminished liability. If stock is over-valued in the balance sheet, it will have caused the profit to be over-stated. If inadequate depreciation has been provided on fixed assets, even a loss may be under-stated. Change one entry in the final accounts and another entry must also be changed. This is the fundamental concept of double-entry which we must never forget.

Profit and loss account
Year ended ...

	£	£
Fees received		58,156
Less expenses:		
Salaries	22,147	
Office expenses	11,956	34,103
Net profit for the year		24,053

Balance sheet as at ...

Fixed assets		5,128
Current assets		
Debtor	752	
Cash	512	
	1,264	
Current liability		
Creditor	152	
Net current assets		1,112
Net assets		6,240
Capital account		
Balance brought forward	14,137	
Add Net profit for the year	24,053	
	38,190	
Less Drawings	31,950	6,240

Figure 36. Profit and loss account and balance sheet derived from the trial balance given earlier

13 Specimen questions and answers

Question 1

(a) How would you distinguish between capital expenditure and revenue expenditure?

(b) State, with reasons, in which of the two categories you would place each of the following items:

(i) cost of repairs to plant, £792;

(ii) cost of an addition to an existing machine which will improve its performance, £600;

(iii) cost of repairing and replacing woodwork, which had been destroyed by woodworm in a building which had been in the same ownership since it was built, £2,000.

Would it make any difference to your answer if you were told that the building had been purchased recently, and its state was known when the contract to buy was signed?

Answer 1

(a) Capital expenditure is that which produces or improves an asset of enduring value, the benefits from which will be obtained over a lengthy period (usually several or many years). It is expenditure to provide the means of earning the profit. Revenue expenditure is on day-to-day operations, and the benefit will be fully obtained in a short period of time, e.g. salaries for the week or month, rent for the quarter. It includes all expenditure to maintain assets in their existing condition.

(b) (i) Repairs to plant £792 will be revenue expenditure since it will merely restore the plant to its previous condition and the cost of such repairs must fall against the revenue of the period in which such repairs become necessary.

(ii) The cost of the addition to an existing machine will be capital expenditure, since the benefits will be reaped over a long period.

(iii) The cost of repairing and replacing woodwork will be revenue expenditure, for the same reasons as are given in (i) above. If the building had been purchased recently in a dilapidated condition, the expenditure should then be regarded as capital, since it is improving the asset which would have been purchased cheap because of its poor state of repair.

Question 2

Give a brief explanation of:

(a) the accountancy procedures for recording the capitalisation of retained profit; and
(b) the financial benefits a company receives from profit retention.

Answer 2

(a) In the case of sole traders and partnerships, retained profits may be capitalised quite simply by adding them to the proprietor's capital account, and there are no legal formalities. In the case of a limited company there will be a debit to the profit and loss account and a credit to a capital reserve, or more usually, to the share capital account. If a bonus or capitalisation issue of shares is to be made in this way, the authorised share capital of the company may need to be increased and the new issue of shares will be to members in proportion to their existing shareholdings. These actions will need to be approved by the members in general meeting, additional share certificates issued to members, and all these events reported to the Registrar of Companies on the appropriate company forms.

(b) Profit retained by a company increases the permanent capital of the enterprise. Not only does it enable expansion to take place, but also the employment of more funds should in turn lead to greater profits. These in turn will produce greater liquidity, perhaps enabling borrowed funds to be repaid and so saving interest charges. The retention of profit therefore broadens the base of the company and leads to greater financial stability and greater profits.

Question 3
The summarised balance sheet of Kilmore Ltd at 31 December, 19–1 was as follows:

Balance sheet – 31 December 19–1

	£	£
Fixed assets at cost	38,000	
Less depreciation	11,240	26,760
Current assets	26,488	
Less current liabilities	11,032	15,456
		42,216
Debentures		10,000
		32,216
Share capital and reserves		
Share capital	25,000	
Profit and loss account	7,216	32,216

Note: A dividend of £2,000 was approved for 19–1. This has been provided for and is included in current liabilities in the balance sheet.

The summarised profit and loss account for 19–2 is shown on the next page.

A dividend of £2,250 was proposed for 19–2 and a transfer of £5,000 to general reserve was approved. The current liabilities, excluding the dividend payable, were £1,000 more at 31 December 19–2 than they were at 31 December 19–1. No fixed assets were bought in 19–2 and no shares or debentures were issued during the year.

	£	£
Sales		279,306
Cost of sales		204,219
Gross profit		75,087
Less expenses		
General expenses	62,498	
Debenture interest	600	
Depreciation	4,675	67,773
Net profit		7,314

Required:
(a) Kilmore's appropriation account for 19–2;
(b) a calculation of Kilmore's current assets at 31 December 19–2;
(c) a summarised balance sheet at 31 December 19–2 in the same form as that appearing above.
Note: Ignore taxation.

Answer 3

(a)

Appropriation Account
Year ended 31 December 19–2

	£	£
Net profit for the year		7,314
Less Transfer to general reserve	5,000	
Proposed dividend	2,250	7,250
Retained profits for the year		64
Retained profits brought forward		7,216
Retained profits carried forward		7,280

(b)

Calculation of current assets at 31 December 19–2:

	£	£
Current assets at 31 December 19-1		26,488
Net profit for 19–2	7,314	
Less dividend for 19–2	2,250	5,064
Depreciation charge for 19–2		4,675
		36,227
Add increase in current liabilities and dividend		1,250
Total at 31 December 19–2		37,477

(c)

Balance sheet – 31 December 19–2

	£	£
Fixed assets, at cost	38,000	
Less depreciation	15,915	22,085
Current assets	37,477	
Less current liabilities	12,282	25,195
		47,280
Debentures		10,000
		37,280
Share capital and reserves		
Share capital	25,000	
General reserve	5,000	
Profit and loss account	7,280	37,280

Note: Current liabilities comprise:

Total at 31 December 19-1	11,032
Increase as given	1,000
Increase in dividend	250
	12,282

Question 4

Explain the significance of the terms 'provision' and 'reserve' in the context of the accounts of a limited company. Why is it important to distinguish between them in a balance sheet?

Answer 4

A *provision* is an amount set aside to meet a known liability or diminution in value (e.g. depreciation) the amount of which cannot be determined with substantial accuracy at the balance sheet date.

A *reserve* comprises profits retained in the business as augmentation of proprietor's capital: they are the source of funds for the expansion of the business.

The importance of distinguishing between them is that provisions are usually liabilities which must be paid in cash (or losses in value which will be replaced by the purchase of fresh fixed assets): reserves are long term additional funds in the business, and are grouped with the shareholders' other funds, such as share capital and profit and loss account.

Question 5

On 1 January 19–3, John Smith purchased six machines for £1,500 each. His accounting year ends on 31 December. Depreciation at the rate of 10% per annum on cost has been charged against income each year and credited to the provision for depreciation account.

On 1 January 19–4, one machine was sold for £1,250 and on 1 January 19–5, a second machine was sold for £1,150. An improved machine which cost £2,800 was purchased on 1 July 19–4. Depreciation was charged on this new machine at the same rate as that on earlier purchases.

Required:

(a) the machinery account and the provision for depreciation account for 19–3, 19–4 and 19–5; and

(b) the entry for machines in the balance sheet at 31 December 19–5.

Answer 5

(a)

Machinery Account

		£			£
1/1/–3	Cost (6)	9,000	1/1/–4	Sales proceeds	1,250
1/7/–4	Cost (1)	2,800	1/1/–4	Depreciation	150
			31/12/–4	Profit & Loss A/c – loss	100
			31/12/–4	Balance carried down	10,300
		11,800			11,800
1/1/–5	Balance brought down	10,300	1/1/–5	Sale proceeds	1,150
			1/1/–5	Depreciation	300
			31/12/–5	Profit & Loss A/c – loss	50
			31/12/–5	Balance carried down	8,800
		10,300			10,300
1/1/–6	Balance brought down	8,800			

Provision for Depreciation of Machinery

		£			£
1/1/–4	Transfer, machinery A/c	150	31/12/–3	Profit & Loss A/c	900
31/12/–4	Balance carried down	1,640	31/12/–4	Profit & Loss A/c	890
		1,790			1,790
1/1/–5	Transfer, machinery A/c	300	1/1/–5	Balance brought down	1,640
31/12/–5	Balance carried down	2,220	31/12/–5	Profit & Loss A/c	880
		2,520			2,520
			1/1/–6	Balance brought down	2,220

(b)

Entry in balance sheet at 31 December 19–5

	£	£
Fixed assets:		
Machinery, at cost	8,800	
Less Provision for depreciation	2,220	6,580

Question 6

On 31 December, 19–7, the whole of the stock of Jackson, a trader, was destroyed by fire.

The following information is available from his books.

	£
Debtors for sales, 31 December 19–6	8,683
Creditors for purchases, 31 December 19–6	8,249
Debtors for sales, 31 December 19–7	9,427
Creditors for purchases, 31 December 19–7	6,236
Payments to suppliers in 19–7	70,448
Receipts from customers in 19–7	91,224
Stock in trade, 31 December 19–6	10,642

Jackson sells all his goods at a price which gives him a fixed gross profit rate of 25% on sales.

Required:
A calculation, on the basis of the above information, of the value of stock that was lost in the fire on 31 December 19–7.

Answer 6

Sales in 19–7	£	£
Receipts from customers in 19–7	91,224	
Less debtors at 1 January	8,683	
	82,541	
Add debtors at 31 December	9,427	91,968
Purchases in 19–7		
Payments to suppliers	70,448	
Less creditors at 1 January	8,249	
	62,199	
Add creditors at 31 December	6,236	68,435
Stock		
Stock in trade, 1 January	10,642	
Add purchases as above	68,435	
	79,077	
Less 75% of sales as above (i.e. the cost of the goods sold)	68,976	
Value of stock at 31 December lost in the fire	10,101	

Question 7
The balance sheet of Ebb Tide Ltd, a construction company, at 31 December 19–7 was as follows:

Balance sheet

	£	£
Fixed assets		
Land and buildings at cost		100,000
Plant at cost	221,000	
Less depreciation	59,970	161,030
		261,030
Current assets		
Raw materials	26,869	
Work in progress	113,031	
Debtors	88,428	
Cash at bank	1,675	
	230,003	
Creditors: amounts falling due within one year		
Creditors for raw materials	31,854	
Accrued expenses	9,061	
Dividend for 19–7	15,000	
	55,915	
Net current assets		174,088
		435,118
Creditors: amounts falling due after more than one year		
9% Debentures		100,000
Net assets		335,118
Share capital and reserves		
Paid-up share capital	150,000	
Profit and loss account	185,118	335,118

During 19–8:

(a) raw materials costing £280,174 were purchased;
(b) wages paid were £310,601;

(c) general expenses paid were £10,593;
(d) £665,528 was received from customers for completed contracts
(e) raw materials charged to contracts amounted to £215,984; all wages were charged to contracts;
(f) the dividend for 19–7, £15,000, and debenture interest for 19–8 were paid;
(g) the charge for depreciation on plant for 19–8 was £31,150;

At 31 December 19–8:

(h) creditors for raw materials were £41,279 and for general expenses £4,218;
(i) work in progress was valued at £95,400 and debtors amounted to £82,500;
(j) a dividend of £16,000 was proposed for 19–8.

Ebb Tide Ltd passed all receipts and payments through its bank account.

Required:

(i) the bank account for 19–8 in the books of Ebb Tide Ltd;
(ii) the profit and loss account for 19–8 and a balance sheet as at 31 December 19–8.

Note: Ignore taxation.

Answer 7

Bank Account
Year ended 31 December 19–8

	£		£
Balance brought down	1,675	Raw materials (280,174 + 31,854 – 41,279)	270,749
Completed contracts	665,528	Wages	310,601
		General expenses	10,593
		Dividend 19–7	15,000
		Debenture interest	9,000
		Balance carried down	51,260
	667,203		667,203

Profit and Loss Account
Year ended 31 December 19–8

	£	£
Turnover (665,528 + 82,500 – 88,428)	659,600	
Add Work in progress, 31 December 19–8	95,400	
	755,000	
Less Work in progress, 1 January 19–8	113,031	641,969
Cost of sales:		
Purchases	280,174	
Add Stock, 1 January 19–8	26,869	
	307,043	
Less Stock, 31 December 19–8 (280,174 – 215,984)	64,190	
	242,853	
Wages	310,601	553,454
Gross profit		88,515
Less expenses:		
General expenses (10,593 + 4,218 – 9,061)	5,750	
Depreciation	31,150	
Debenture interest	9,000	45,900
Net profit for the year		42,615
Less proposed dividend		16,000
Retained profit for the year		26,615
Retained profits brought forward		185,118

Balance sheet - 31 March 19–8

	£	£
Fixed assets		
Land and buildings at cost		100,000
Plant at cost	221,000	
Less depreciation (59,970 + 31,150)	91,120	129,880
		229,880
Current assets		
Raw materials	64,190	
Work in progress	95,400	
Debtors	82,500	
Cash at bank	51,260	
	293,350	
Creditors: amounts falling due within one year		
Creditors for raw materials	41,279	
Accrued expenses	4,218	
Dividend	16,000	
	61,497	
Net current assets		231,853
		461,733
Creditors: amounts falling due after more than one year		
9% Debentures		100,000
Net assets		361,733
Share capital and reserves		
Paid-up share capital	150,000	
Profit and loss account	211,733	361,733

Question 8

A company balance sheet shows one account for ordinary share capital irrespective of the number of shareholders; a separate capital account for each partner is reported in the balance sheet of a partnership. Explain the reason for and the advantages of this difference in treatment.

Answer 8

A company is a separate legal entity whereas a partnership is an association of individuals. The profits earned by a company belong to it, and may be withdrawn as dividends only if and when such are recommended by the directors. The profits earned by a partnership are divisible in a predetermined ratio between the partners and, subject to any restriction in the partnership agreement, may be withdrawn by the partners in differing amounts and at different dates. The amount of the company's paid-up share capital may only be reduced by an elaborate procedure involving the approval of creditors and the sanction of the court: but partners may vary the amounts of their capital in a firm subject only to mutual agreement.

The difference in treatment between the capital of a company and that of a partnership stems from the fact that company rules are made for large organisations, and these must entail a certain inflexibility. Thus each shareholder is treated the same as regards calls on shares and dividends payable, subject only to the difference in the number of shares held.

The number of partners permitted in a partnership has traditionally been limited to 20, reduced to 10 in the case of banking: although these rules have now been relaxed in the case of professions, this tradition of small numbers has made it practicable to keep a high measure of flexibility and maintain a separate capital (and perhaps current account as well) for each partner. Every partner has a voice in the management of a partnership, whilst shareholders delegate their powers to the directors, and their voices are heard only at general meetings.

Both systems have inherent advantages and in most types of business activity the entrepreneur may select which type of organisation to use.

Question 9

Arthur Glenton is the proprietor of a small but long-established manufacturing business. The summarised accounts for the year 19–9 are as follows:

Profit and loss account

	£	£
Sales		200,000
Variable cost of sales		120,000
Gross profit		80,000
Less expenses:		
General expenses	43,000	
Depreciation	17,000	60,000
Net profit		20,000

Balance sheet as at 31 December 19–9

	£	£
Fixed assets at cost	170,000	
Less depreciation	80,000	90,000
Current assets	50,000	
Less current liabilities	26,000	24,000
		114,000
Capital account		
Balance brought forward	110,000	
Add net profit for the year	20,000	
	130,000	
Less drawings	16,000	114,000

The financial results of the business have shown little change in recent years, and the financial position has been very stable, supported by the fact that annual drawings have generally been materially lower than the profit. The expectation is that there will be little change over the next few years and that the level of profit will be maintained.

Glenton has recently been invited to increase his production to meet an export demand in a market where the prospects of development and increased sales are very substantial. Additional plant with a 10-year life will be needed for such an expansion. Plant units which will produce £40,000 of sales per annum are available at

£36,000 per unit.

The variable cost of sales for the export market will be 65% of the overseas selling price; the gross profit for inland sales will be unchanged. Additional general expenses will amount to £10,000 for the first £40,000 increase in sales, but will fall to £4,000 for each £40,000 block of additional sales above the first £40,000.

Glenton has no private resources. The existing liquid resources of the business would cover the additional working capital required, and also provide £10,000 towards the capital cost of the new project. A finance company is prepared to lend up to £100,000 to Glenton at 15% per annum.

An alternative proposal is made to Glenton. Mumford Ltd offers him £120,000 in cash for the business and is prepared to retain his services as manager on a 10-year contract at a salary of £14,000 per annum plus an additional £1,000 per annum for each £20,000 increase in turnover.

Required:

(a) Statements reporting on the profit likely to be received from overseas sales at the rate of £20,000, £40,000 and £60,000 per annum respectively.

(b) A report for Glenton in which you discuss the prospects of the new venture, explaining the reasons for the difference in the expected profit, and finally advising him what to do.

Note: Glenton can expect to invest the proceeds of the sale of his business at 10% per annum.

Answer 9

	£	£	£	£	£	£
Additional sales		40,000		80,000		120,000
Less variable cost (65%)		26,000		52,000		78,000
Gross profit		14,000		28,000		42,000
Less:						
Additional general expenses	10,000		14,000		18,000	
Additional depreciation	3,600		7,200		10,800	
Loan interest	3,900	17,500	9,300	30,500	14,700	43,500
Loss		3,500		2,500		1,500

(a) Increase in profits from additional overseas sales
(b) Effect of accepting offer from Mumford Ltd

	Present sales level	+£40,000	+£80,000	+£120,000
	£	£	£	£
Salary	14,000	16,000	18,000	20,000
Interest on £120,000 at 10%	12,000	12,000	12,000	12,000
	26,000	28,000	30,000	32,000

It is clear that Arthur Glenton would be considerably better off by accepting the offer from Mumford Ltd as it would increase his income by £6,000 at the present level of sales. If he installs the additional machinery to meet his export demand, he is actually going to reduce his net profit as the loan interest will more than offset his additional profits.

Therefore the advice to Arthur Glenton would be to accept the offer of Mumford Ltd and not to attempt to increase the sales by way of the export market.

Question 10

The balance sheets of Tintop Ltd at 31 December 20–1 and 20–2 may be summarised as follows:

		20–1		20–2
	£	£	£	£
Fixed assets at cost		202,000		245,000
Less depreciation		83,000		105,000
		119,000		140,000
Current assets				
Stock	25,000		50,000	
Debtors	23,000		29,000	
Cash at bank	12,000		1,000	
	60,000		80,000	
Less current liabilities	30,000	30,000	37,000	43,000
		149,000		183,000
Share capital	100,000		100,000	
Retained profits	49,000	149,000	83,000	183,000

The figure of current liabilities at 31 December 20–1 includes a proposed dividend of £5,000 for the year to date. No decision has been taken yet about the dividend to be paid for 20–2, and nothing is included in the 20–2 balance sheet for such dividend.

The directors are considering the dividend that should be paid for 20–2 in the light of the excellent results for that year.

Required:

(a) A calculation of the maximum dividend that should be declared for 20–2 if the working capital ratio in the December 20–2 balance sheet is to be the same as in the December 20–1 balance sheet.
(b) A brief discussion of the financial policy pursued by the directors of Tintop Ltd in 20–2.

Note: Ignore taxation.

Answer 10

(a) The ratio of working capital is Current assets/current liabilities x 100
For 20–1 this is £60,000/ £30,000 x 100 = 200%.
For 20–2 the ratio will be 200% if the liabilities are £40,000 with current assets £80,000.

As current liabilities excluding any dividend are already £37,000, this would mean that the dividend would be only £3,000 against £5,000 the previous year, although the profits before dividend for 20–2 were £34,000 (retained profits £83,000 – previous year £49,000).

(b) The financial policy of the directors of Tintop Ltd (so far as can be deduced from the limited information supplied) appears to be that the purchase of fixed assets is financed from profits, and that working capital ratio must be maintained if necessary by curtailing the dividend payment to shareholders.

The priorities for utilisation of funds appears to be (1) fixed assets; (2) working capital; (3) dividends. If this policy is pursued over several years, the shareholders may well feel that they are being neglected! And if the directors do not hold a majority of the shares, the shareholders may feel a change of directors should be considered!

A funds flow statement for the year 20–2 shows the position clearly:

	£	£
Profit for the year	34,000	
Depreciation	22,000	56,000
Applied to:		
Purchase of fixed assets	43,000	
Additional working capital	10,000	
Dividend	3,000	56,000

Question 11

The balance sheet of the Freebooters Club at 31 December 20–0 is as follows:

Balance sheet

	£	£
Fixed assets		
Investments at cost	22,300	
Furniture and equipment, at cost less depreciation	7,600	29,900
Current assets		
Bar stocks	2,050	
Cash at bank	3,570	
	5,620	
Current liabilities		
Creditors for bar purchases	1,020	
Accrued expenses	40	
	1,060	
Net current assets		4,560
Net assets		34,460
Accumulated fund		34,460

A summary of the club's bank account for 20–1 is as follows:
On 31 December 20–1, bar stocks were valued at £2,984 and £1,142

	£		£
Balance at 1 January	3,570	Bar purchases	40,190
Subscriptions received	13,100	Wages and salaries	24,210
Bar sales	66,650	Rent and rates	8,200
Investment income	2,080	General expenses	6,440
		Cost of new investments	5,000
		Balance at 31 December	1,360
	85,400		85,4002

was owing for bar supplies; £62 was owing for expenses.

The owner of the building of which the club occupies a part proposes to sell it for £85,000; he has offered it to the trustees of the club and they are considering the proposal.

The investments held by the club could be sold for £54,000 and a member of the club has offered to lend £10,000 at 5% per annum for five years. The secretary of the club has approached the bank to negotiate an overdraft for the balance needed to purchase the building. The bank has asked to see the 20–1 accounts and wishes to have an estimate of the amount that will be available annually for repayment.

Part of the building is occupied by a second organisation which pays its own rates and from which the present owner receives an annual rent of £1,000. The club will remain liable for the rates on the part of the building it occupies amounting to £900 per annum.

There are no subscriptions in arrears or in advance. Depreciation should be charged on the furniture and equipment at the rate of 10% per annum on the figure shown in the balance sheet at 31 December 20–0.

Required:

(a) A bar trading account and an income and expenditure account for 20–1 and a balance sheet at the end of that year.
(b) A calculation showing:

(i) the maximum amount to be borrowed on overdraft, as at 1 January 20–2, to meet the cost of the building; and
(ii) the annual surplus that will be available to meet the interest on the overdraft for repayment on the assumption that the 20–1 results are repeated in each of the following five years.

Note: (1) Ignore taxation.
(2) There was no capital expenditure during 20–1.
(3) Allow £1,000 for legal costs of purchase of the premises.

Answer 11

(a)

Bar Trading Account
Year ended 31 December 20–1

	£	£
Bar sales		66,650
Cost of sales		
Stock, 1 January 20–1	2,050	
Add purchases		
(40,190 – 1,020 + 1,142)	40,312	
	42,362	
Less Stock 31 December 20–1	2,984	
	39,378	
Wages and salaries	24,210	63,588
Gross profit, carried to I & E Account		3,062

Income and Expenditure Account
Year ended 31 December 20–1

	£	£
Subscriptions		13,100
Gross profit on bar trading		3,062
Investment income		2,080
		18,242
Less Rent and rates	8,200	
General expenses		
(6,440 – 40 + 62)	6,462	
Depreciation	760	15,422
Surplus for the year		2,820

Balance Sheet – 31 December 20–1

	£	£
Fixed assets		
Investments at cost		27,300
Furniture and equipment		
at cost less depreciation		
(7,600 – 760)		6,840
		34,140
Current assets		
Bar stocks	2,984	
Cash at bank	1,360	
	4,344	
Current liabilities		
Creditors for bar purchases	1,142	
Accrued expenses	62	
	1,204	
Net current assets		3,140
Net assets		37,280
Accumulated fund		
Balance at 1 January 20–1	34,460	
Add Surplus for year	2,820	37,280

(b) (i) *Maximum amount to be borrowed on overdraft as at 1 January 20–1*

Cost of building			£85,000
Legal costs on purchase			1,000
			86,000
Less	Financed by investments now sold	54,000	
	Financed by member's loan	10,000	64,000
			£22,000

The current bank balance (£1,360) will presumably be required to meet creditors (£1,204) assumed all now due.

It would therefore seem that £22,000 should be borrowed from the bank, but this could be reduced if, as is likely, members' subscriptions are due on 1 January 20–2, many of which may be payable under direct debit or standing order arrangements: this reduction could be £5,000 or £6,000, particularly as the previous year showed a cash surplus of £5,000 which was placed in additional investments.

(ii) Annual surplus that will be available to meet interest and repayment

Surplus as 20–1			£2,820
Add	rent now saved (£8,200 – £900)	7,300	
	rent receivable	1,000	
	depreciation charge (which does not involve cash payment)	760	9,060
			11,880
Less	investment income lost	2,080	
	interest on loan (5% on £10,000)	500	2,580
Available for interest and repayment			£9,300

Question 12

The cash balance of Wing Ltd has declined significantly over the last twelve months. The following financial information is provided.

Year to 31 December	20–3 £	20–4 £
Sales	573,000	643,000
Purchases of raw materials	215,000	264,000
Raw materials consumed	210,000	256,000
Cost of goods manufactured	435,000	515,000
Cost of goods sold	420,000	460,000
Balance at 31 December	**20–3**	**20–4**
Debtors	97,100	121,500
Creditors	23,900	32,500
Stocks: Raw materials	22,400	30,000
Work in progress	29,000	34,300
Finished goods	70,000	125,000

All purchases and sales were made on credit.

Required:

(a) An analysis of the above information, which should include calculations of the cash operating cycle (i.e. the time lag between making payments to suppliers and collecting cash from customers) for 20–3 and 20–4.
(b) A brief report on the implications of the changes which have occurred between 20–3 and 20–4.

Note: 1. Assume a 360-day year for the purpose of your calculations, and that all transactions take place at an even rate.
2. All calculations are to be made to the nearest day.

Answer 12

	20–3	20–4
Stocks of raw materials		
£22,400/£210,000 x 360	38 days	
£30,000/£256,400 x 360		42 days
Credit given by suppliers		
£23,900/£215,000 x 360	Credit 40 days	
£32,500/£264,000 x 360		Credit 44 days
Work in progress		
£29,000/£435,000 x 360	24 days	
£34,300/£515,000 x 360		24 days
Stock of finished goods		
£70,000/£420,000 x 360	60 days	
£125,000/£460,000 x 360		98 days
Debtors		
£97,100/£573,000 x 360	61 days	
£121,500/£643,000 x 360		68 days
Cash operating cycle	143 days	188 days

(b) The cash operating cycle has increased in the second year from 143 days to 188 days. This has arisen through the stock of finished goods increasing from 60 days, to 98 days usage, and from the debtors increasing from the equivalent of 61 days' sales to 68 days' sales. If the assumption made that all transactions have taken place at an even rate is well founded, attention needs to be given to reducing the amount of stock of finished goods held, and also to the tightening of credit controls on sales.

Index